CLEVELAND INDIANS

The Cleveland Press Years

1920–1982

D1603870

MINNIE MINOSO IS SAFE AT THE PLATE, JULY 1959. Running hard on Tito Francona's hit to right field, Minoso scores as Baltimore catcher Joe Ginsberg drops the ball. Umpire Jim Honochick makes the call.

CLEVELAND INDIANS

The Cleveland Press Years

1920–1982

To the Hudson Library
with my very best wishes —

[signature]

November 1, 2003

David Borsvold

ARCADIA

Copyright © 2003 by David Borsvold.
ISBN 0-7385-2325-9

Published by Arcadia Publishing,
an imprint of Tempus Publishing, Inc.
2 Cumberland Street
Charleston, SC 29401

Printed in Great Britain.

Library of Congress Catalog Card Number: 2003101432

For all general information contact Arcadia Publishing at:
Telephone 843-853-2070
Fax 843-853-0044
E-Mail sales@arcadiapublishing.com

For customer service and orders:
Toll-Free 1-888-313-2665

Visit us on the internet at http://www.arcadiapublishing.com

To my parents, Herb and Mary Borsvold

OSCAR GAMBLE LEADS THE TEAM BACK TO THE DUGOUT AFTER AN 11TH-INNING GAME-WINNING HOMER IN 1972.

CONTENTS

ACKNOWLEDGMENTS

The photographs in this book came from a single source, the Special Collections in the University Library at Cleveland State University. I first became aware of the size and scope of the *Cleveland Press* archive that is housed there in 2002, when they kindly allowed me to reproduce several dozen images for a book about Ashtabula, Ohio published by Arcadia.

The Special Collections is an archive which sets the standard in terms of access, professionalism and courtesy. I am very grateful to Special Collections Librarian William C. Barrow for allowing me to spend many hours covering a library table with a photo scanner and other equipment, and to Joanne Cornelius, Lynn Duchez Bycko and Bill Becker for bringing mountains of photos to me upon request. A special note of thanks goes to Mr. Becker who, without being asked, offered to let me stay well past closing time on my final day there, saving me a great deal of travel.

It is important to note that none of the Special Collections staff has had any input into, nor bears any responsibility for, the written content of the book. A tremendous amount of well-organized Cleveland area historical information and photography may be seen on their website at:

http://web.ulib.csuohio.edu/SpecColl/

I am grateful also to Bob Sudyk, *Cleveland Press* baseball writer from 1965 to '82, who took an interest in the book and kindly answered several questions for me.

In researching the history of the team, I was greatly helped by reading David Kaiser's *Epic Season: The 1948 American League Pennant Race*; Terry Pluto's *The Curse of Rocky Colavito: A Loving Look at a Thirty-Year Slump* and *Our Tribe: A Baseball Memoir*; Bill Veeck's *Veeck as in Wreck*; and two books by Russell Schneider, *The Boys of the Summer of '48* and, especially, *The Cleveland Indians Encyclopedia*, the essential volume for anyone more than casually interested in the Tribe.

INTRODUCTION

Six division titles in seven years. Two American League pennants! Who would have believed it?

When the Cleveland Indians spectacularly returned to contention in 1994, after thirty-four years of purgatory in which the supreme achievement was their third-place finish of 1968, the impact was undoubtedly greatest upon Cleveland baseball fans born between 1960 and 1980. We marveled at the luxurious new Jacobs Field, the annual winter rush to buy tickets, the record run of consecutive sellouts, and the national recognition of the suddenly-hip Indians. But most of all, we reveled in winning baseball, a new crop of stars, and the annual postseason excitement. Once again, the Indians ruled in Cleveland sports, and a connection was made with the generation that remembered the 1948 Championship and the consistent excellence of the Fifties.

Cleveland fans born after the early Eighties simply have not suffered enough to appreciate what it means to have a winning baseball team.

Although the Cleveland franchise was founded along with the American League just over a century ago, the Indians have won only two World Series championships, in 1920 and 1948. They contended regularly during most of the 1950s, won a (then) league-record 111 games in 1954 but were swept in the Series by the New York Giants, and put competitive, exciting teams on the field through 1959. But the high times ended on the eve of the 1960 season, when young superstar outfielder Rocky Colavito was traded away. Baseball slumbered painfully in the city from 1960 through 1993, due to a dreary succession of mediocre teams, and the public's loyalty and interest were measured by the low attendance at the ballpark. The perceived reasons for losing rotated regularly, and often overlapped: bad pitching, bad hitting, bad fielding, inexplicable trades, horrible luck and real tragedies, the major leagues' worst stadium, strife-torn management, a weak farm system, and a lack of cash. In most years the season was over by June—if not May. Hope sprang eternal, of course. If the Tribe got off to a strong start in the spring, words like "contender" and "first place" briefly crossed fans' lips as they raced down to the Municipal Stadium turnstiles for the start of a homestand, usually just in time to witness a lights-out sweep by the Tigers or the Yankees that would put an end to such talk.

For me, the most enduring vignette of the losing years is a drizzly night half-remembered from sometime during the Eighties. With the Indians trailing in the bottom of the fifth, and a chilly breeze stiffening to the accompaniment of weakly rolling thunder, Brook Jacoby struck out to end the inning (five being the minimum number of innings to count in the record book as a complete game). Before Jacoby even made it back to the dugout, the drizzle, which had shown signs of strengthening, abruptly turned to a hard cold rain that descended in thick ropes. Despite the delightful prospect of earlier-than-usual postgame food and drink, the umpires would have to wait a little while before calling the game, but those few fans present knew the truth as certainly as if a voice had spoken from the dark skies: "This Game Is Over!"

Even with the countless stranded baserunners, two-out rallies killed by fly balls to the warning track, and batters failing to run out ground balls, it wasn't all bad by any means. Indians baseball was the most affordable and accessible summer ticket in Cleveland. In general, we went down to the games on a beautiful July evening with limited goals: general enjoyment, a nice breeze off Lake Erie, a cold beer, giveaways, the chance to see visiting stars such as Carl Yasztremski, Brooks Robinson, or Reggie Jackson, possibly even a Tribe win and some fireworks out of the centerfield bleachers. The poor sound system, miscellaneous flying bugs, lousy bathrooms, and hard wooden seats at the ancient Stadium simply meant that "you get what you pay for." Even if one weren't lucky enough to witness Eckersley's no-hitter or Barker's perfect game, there was a lot to be said for sitting right behind home plate, eating and drinking, and watching Bert Blyleven throw his booming curveball all night. Perhaps Andre Thornton would launch a ball over the fence to provide a little electricity. Driving home, we could listen to "Sportsline" host Pete Franklin breaking it all down. And over breakfast we would read about it, and see it in pictures, in the newspaper.

This book contains newspaper photographs spanning sixty-two seasons of the Cleveland Indians, including the great years of the Forties and Fifties, and less successful (but always colorful) campaigns of the 1920s, 30s, 60s, 70s and early 80s. During the first six decades of the twentieth century, there were three competing daily newspapers in Cleveland: the *Cleveland News*, the *Cleveland Plain Dealer*, and the *Cleveland Press*, and each sent writers and photographers to cover the baseball games. On Jan. 23, 1960, the *Cleveland News* was purchased by and merged with the *Press*, leaving just two dailies to compete in coverage.

The *Cleveland Press* had been launched as the *Penny Press* in 1878 by Edward Willis Scripps (1854-1926). As the first newspaper founded and owned by Scripps, the *Penny Press* was the cornerstone

FLAG RAISING AT LEAGUE PARK, OPENING DAY 1924.

of a growing publishing empire. When E. W. Scripps died at 71, his Scripps-Howard organization owned twenty-five newspapers; in the years to come it would acquire and operate broadcast outlets as well. Scripps had also created United Press International, a competitor to the Associated Press, and the Newspaper Enterprise Association, a syndication service that was a precursor to United Media. The *Cleveland Press* reached the peak of its reputation in the mid-twentieth century under the editorship of the legendary Louis B. Seltzer, a larger-than-life mover and shaker in the community.

To judge by contemporary written accounts, the *Press* seems to have been a true family, full of memorable characters and normal dysfunction but also a shared sense of mission and purpose. Former staffers Dick Feagler, Ray DeCrane, and others have written eloquently about the unique experience of working for the *Press* in its final decades, and some of these reminiscences are available today on the Internet (see the Acknowledgements on Page 127).

Seltzer retired in 1966, and it was not long before financial woes began to plague the newspaper. After enduring difficult times through the Seventies, the 102-year-old *Cleveland Press* was sold to Cleveland industrialist Joseph E. Cole on October 31, 1980. Less than two years later the *Press* folded, and Cleveland was consigned to the dreary status of a "one-newspaper town." The main competition for Cleveland sports coverage now came from an out-of-town paper, the *Akron Beacon Journal*. The *Press*'s baseball writer from 1965 to 1982, Bob Sudyk (shown on page 9), went on to a fine career at the *Hartford Courant* in Connecticut, writing on many topics beyond sports. His byline is again appearing in Cleveland-area publications today.

A great many of the *Cleveland Press* baseball photographs, dating from the 1920s until 1982 (the newspaper's last year of operation), are preserved in the Special Collections at the Cleveland State University Library, which administers the entire 500,000-photograph archive donated in 1984 by the newspaper's owner (and then-CSU Trustee), Mr. Cole. A few of the baseball images—such as Gene Bearden being carried off the field after the 1948 playoff victory, or Paul Tepley's photo of Dennis Eckersley leaping into the arms of catcher Ray Fosse after completing a no-hitter—have received wide exposure and become classics. Most of the others have not been seen in print since they first ran in the *Press*.

This book showcases the work of photographers Herman Seid, Diana McMees, Ron Kuntz, L. Van Deyen, and others; Paul Tepley's outstanding images dominate the later decades. The exact dates of some photos are difficult to determine, and in the early decades the photographers' names were very rarely recorded. Most of the photos which survive from the 1920s are informal posed group portraits rather than game action shots, but with each passing decade the variety improves. It is impossible to know what never made it to the Special Collections, as undoubtedly some of the best photos were spirited away in earlier years. There are no game photos from the 1920 World Series, and while there is some coverage of the two Series appearances of 1948 and 1954, action photos from those games are scarce. Len Barker is in the collection, but his perfect game is not. Some Indians (Bob Feller, for instance) are very well represented, while a few familiar players are almost, or entirely, absent. Some of the older prints are simply in too poor condition to reproduce, and others were rather grotesquely retouched to compensate for the low-contrast newspaper photo reproduction of the era.

The material that remains is wonderful to browse through, and narrowing the selection down to 180 images was difficult. This collection presents many of the best photos that are still extant, organizing them chronologically. Not only are most of the great Indians players shown, but some legendary opposing players—Ruth, Gehrig, DiMaggio, Molitor, Rod Carew, Frank Howard, Ted Williams—are seen in rare and precious photographs from Cleveland Stadium.

Each chapter begins with a summary of the team's fortunes during the decade that it covers.

CLEVELAND PRESS BASEBALL WRITER BOB SUDYK WITH PITCHER RALPH TERRY IN MAY 1965.

ONE

The 1920s

The Roaring Twenties began for baseball with whispers. The 1919 World Series, won by the Cincinnati Reds, had been soured by accusations that eight members of the losing Chicago White Sox—including former Cleveland outfielder "Shoeless Joe" Jackson—had conspired to fix the outcome of the Series at the behest of gamblers. The players confessed to throwing the Fall Classic, yet they would be acquitted at trial's end in 1921. The messy outcome of the case (which included the lifetime banning from the game of all eight men) was still in the future as the Cleveland Indians and the Brooklyn Robins took the field for the 1920 World Series, but suspicion of impropriety hung over major league baseball like a dark cloud.

In addition, the game itself was changing. The pitcher-dominated "dead ball era," during which batters choked up on heavy bats and tried to punch the softly-wrapped baseball out of the infield, was over. Power hitters were now swinging freely and making contact with a hard ball that soared over the distant outfield fences. Babe Ruth, who had set a major-league record of 29 home runs with Boston in 1919, joined the Yankees and smacked 54 in 1920!

A great Yankees dynasty was ignited with the arrival of Ruth, but that first regular season of the new decade ended with the Cleveland Indians atop the American League. Reaching the 1920 World Series had been an especially difficult achievement for the Cleveland players, who had been wounded by the loss of one of their own. The death of shortstop Ray Chapman in New York on August 16, after being hit in the head by a pitch, shook the team just as deeply as the passing of pitcher Darryl Kile affected the St. Louis Cardinals in 2002. The Tribe dedicated the remainder of their season to the memory of Chapman, and powered to a 98-56 record and the pennant.

The World Series, at that time a best-of-nine tilt, was a seesaw affair through the first four games. Pitcher Stan Coveleski (who earlier in the season had faced an even more personal tragedy, the death of his wife) handcuffed the Brooklyn lineup in a 3-1 Game 1 victory, but the Robins roared back, winning the next two games 3-0 and 2-1. With Coveleski again on the mound in Game 4, the Indians won 5-1, setting up a climactic encounter in the pivotal game in Cleveland's League Park on October 10.

Charlie Jamieson, Bill Wambsganss and Tris Speaker all reached base safely in the first inning of the fifth game, setting the table for outfielder Elmer Smith, who stepped in and launched the ball over the fence for the first-ever grand slam in a World Series. With everybody screaming, the Indians built a 7-0 lead in the fourth inning, before another historic play shut down the Robins' last threat. Brooklyn runners had leads at first and second with no one out when relief pitcher-utilityman Clarence Mitchell hit a rocket, which was caught by Wambsganss at second base. With the runners underway, Wambsganss immediately stepped on the bag to double off Pete Kilduff, then moved quickly to tag a surprised Otto Miller before he could return to first. The startled crowd realized that it had just witnessed an unassisted triple play, the first in World Series history (and to this day the only one).

The 8-1 victory put the Tribe into the driver's seat, and they proceeded to shut out the Robins in Games 6 and 7 to win the franchise's first World Championship. It was a triumphant culmination to the first two decades of existence for the Indians—the successor to two nineteenth-century teams called the Forest Citys and the Spiders—who had gone by several different names since coming into existence along with the American League in 1901: the Blues, Bronchos and finally the Naps, after popular infielder Napoleon Lajoie. Following Lajoie's retirement, a panel of sportswriters had convened with Naps owner Charles Somers in 1915 to select the new team name. "Indians" had been chosen probably in hopes of emulating the 1914 champion Boston Braves, and not, as folkore holds, to honor late-nineteenth century Cleveland player and Native American Louis Sockalexis.

As the Indians prepared to defend their championship in 1921, no player or fan can have imagined that twenty-eight more seasons would pass before the club's next World Series appearance. Competitive all year, the team was hampered by a number of ailments including a late-season knee injury to indispensable center fielder Tris Speaker, and they finished in second place at 94-60. The end of the season had one attraction for Cleveland, however: an exhibition between the AL and NL that was played at League Park on September 28 (though the first All-Star Game was still twelve years in the future).

A four-year slide began in 1922. The Tribe got off to a good start in April, but disappointing pitching and several injuries took a toll. A major distraction was the death of team owner "Sunny Jim" Dunn, which elevated vice president Ernest "Barney" Barnard to president. With a revolving-door roster in which 46 players came and went, the squad slipped to 78-76, 16 games out. The Indians were never in close contention in 1923 either, due again to poor pitching and mediocre fielding. Though their record improved to 82-71, good enough for 3rd place, they still finished 16 1/2 back of the Yankees. The season was enlivened by 23-game hitting streaks by Charlie Jamieson and Tris Speaker, and a league-leading .301 team batting average.

Two disappointing sixth-place place seasons followed. Injuries were again the story in the 1924 campaign which saw the Tribe fall to 67-86, 24 1/2 games back. In December, Stan Coveleski was sent to Washington in a trade which brought little in return and weakened the Tribe's already bad pitching. The team got off to a good start in 1925, battling for first place till mid-May, and then slid out of contention to finish at 70-84. Tris Speaker hit a career-high .389 and got his 3,000th hit on May 17, but fans called for his removal as manager. His contract was extended instead.

1926 was a happier year. The club overcame a rough May through July to contend with the Yankees for first place, closing the gap to three games in the last week of the season, but getting no closer. Still, the second-place 88-66 season, in which first baseman George Burns was selected as American League MVP, raised fans' hopes. Enmeshed in scandal, Tris Speaker both resigned his managership and retired as a player on December 2nd. Speaker and Ty Cobb, who had both been accused of fixing a game in 1919, were later exonerated with a delayed and lukewarm statement from Commissioner Kenesaw Mountain Landis.

The Indians' fortunes again took a turn for the worse in 1927 as they went into free fall under new manager (and former coach) Jack McCallister. Although no team was going to catch the '27 Yankees, the Tribe's sixth-place 66-87 finish sealed McCallister's fate. There were other upheavals around the club: President Barney Barnard became the new American League president, and the team was sold for $1 million to Cleveland real estate executive Alva Bradley and a syndicate of local investors. The new ownership hired AL umpire Billy Evans as GM and Roger Peckinpaugh as field manager. An attempt was made by Bradley to purchase the contract of Lou Gehrig, a Yankees holdout, but Gehrig was hardly to be pried away from New York management.

Despite a 12-6 start in 1928, little improved under the new regime as the Indians slid to a 62-92 finish, 39 games out. After the season, management went looking for better players. Outfielder Earl Averill's contract was purchased from the San Francisco Seals of the Pacific Coast League, and the team also acquired outfielders "Twitchy Dick" Porter and Bibb Falk.

The Great Depression would begin in 1929, and the depression of Indians fans would be but little relieved by a decent 81-71 season in which the team climbed to third place, still 24 games out of first. New players made an impact. Intense fastballer Wes Ferrell, brought up from the minors, began a four-season run of 20-plus wins. First baseman Lew Fonseca, acquired by the club in 1927, came of age with a .369 average and 103 RBI. Averill hit .322, Porter .328, and Falk .312 with 93 RBI.

In November 1928, Cleveland voters had approved the financing of a new $2.5 million downtown ballpark on the lakefront, intended (but not destined) to attract the 1932 Olympics. Due to legal roadblocks, the construction of Municipal Stadium—the largest in baseball—would be delayed until 1930.

"Hustling Dan" O'Leary Visits the Indians. O'Leary played for several National League teams from 1879 to '82, and was a playing manager for the Cincinnati Outlaw Reds in the Union Association in 1884. In this photo from 1920 or 1921, he is accompanied by Tribe pitcher Walter Mails (left) and first baseman George Burns. O'Leary died in 1922.

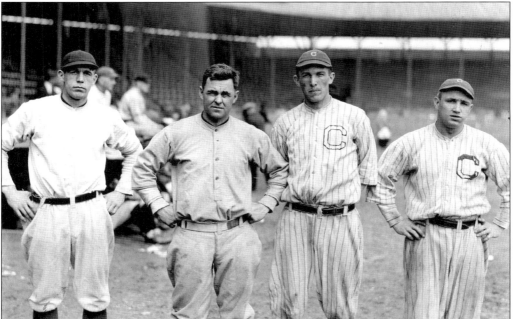

Del Bissonette (left), Stuffy McInnis, Ralph Harwood, and Frank Tubbs in April 1922. Only first baseman McInnis broke camp with the club. Bissonette did not make the Indians' roster, and persevered for nearly a decade before catching on at age 28 with the Brooklyn Dodgers, for whom he hit .305 with 391 RBI from 1928 to '33.

PITCHERS GUY MORTON AND LUTHER ROY IN MAY 1924. Morton (left) racked up a 98-88 record from 1914 to '24, while Roy was much less effective, going 0-5 in 22 appearances in 1924 and 1925. Both were used sparingly during the disappointing 1924 season, a 67-86 effort under manager Tris Speaker.

BILLY EVANS, WASHINGTON NATIONALS PITCHER WALTER JOHNSON, AND BABE RUTH IN MARCH 1925. At this time Evans, a future Tribe GM, was an American League umpire. Johnson would manage the Indians from 1933 to '35.

1926 TEAM PHOTO. Shown here at the end of spring training, the Tribe went on to a very respectable 88-66 second-place finish, three games behind the pennant-winning Yankees. First baseman George Burns was selected as the American League's Most Valuable Player, batting .358 with 4 HR and 111 RBI. Two future Hall of Famers, player-manager Tris Speaker and shortstop Joe Sewell, also turned in stellar performances. Speaker, who would be elected to the Hall of Fame in 1937, batted .304 with 7HR and 86 RBI, though his off-the-field misfortunes would be more memorable. Sewell, who made the trip to Cooperstown in 1977, batted a robust .324 while striking out only six times in 578 at-bats. Second baseman Freddy Spurgeon, third baseman Rube Lutzke, catcher Luke Sewell (Joe's brother), and outfielders Hommer Summa and Charlie Jamieson rounded out the talented day-to-day starters. Right-hander George Uhle went 27-11 with a 2.83 ERA, leading the Indians' pitching staff and the league in victories and winning percentage. Had it not been for Ruth, Gehrig and company, this Tribe club would have met the St. Louis Cardinals in the 1926 World Series.

TWO LITTLE-USED PLAYERS. Pitcher Norm Lehr and third baseman Dutch Ussat are photographed during spring training, March 1926. Lehr (left) would appear in a mere four games during this season, putting up a decent 3.07 ERA on his way to compiling a 0-0 record, while Ussat batted .176 in just five games over two seasons.

LOU GEHRIG AND BABE RUTH, JULY 1927. Judged by many to be the finest team in the history of the game, the '27 Yankees won 110 games and led wire-to-wire, taking the pennant by nineteen games. Their "Murderers Row" lineup was led by Gehrig, who batted .373, and Ruth, who set a major league record with 60 homers; the two combined for 339 RBI. Hitting for power and average, stealing a lot of bases, and shutting down opposing batters, the Yanks regularly squashed the Indians, who finished 43 1/2 games back under manager Jack McCallister.

THE NEW REGIME IN 1928. It had been a busy winter for these three men. Billy Evans (center), a former sportswriter and umpire, was hired as general manager by new team owner Alva Bradley (left). Roger Peckinpaugh, who had played for the Tribe back in the teens, replaced the fired Jack McCallister after the season. He would manage the club until 1933, earning a reputation as a steady and calm leader.

GREAT EXPECTATIONS. Bruce Caldwell, seen here visiting with manager Roger Peckinpaugh, was best known as a football star at Yale University. He was signed by the Indians in 1928 but contributed little, playing in the outfield in eighteen games and batting .222 in his single Tribe campaign. He had a cup of coffee with the 1932 Brooklyn Dodgers, but again made no impact.

THE INDIANS MANAGEMENT STAFF DEPARTING FOR THE 1928 SEASON OPENER IN CHICAGO. After trying fruitlessly to purchase the contract of Yankees holdout Lou Gehrig, the Tribe would limp to a 62-92 record, finishing 39 games back under new manager Roger Peckinpaugh. Waiting to board this Nickel Plate Railroad special, from left to right, are general manager Billy Evans, John Sherwin, Peckinpaugh, Percy Morgan, Joe Hostettler, Frank Hobson, team owner Alva Bradley, Frank O'Brien, and secretary Walter Nichols.

THREE TRIBE PITCHERS IN APRIL
1929. Pictured from left to right are
Jake Miller, Willis Hudlin, and Joe
Shaute. Hudlin threw two shutouts in
1929, a season which saw the Indians
improve drastically to a third-place 81-
71 finish, though without contending
for the pennant.

IMPROVISED SAUNA. Trying to
sweat out the extra pounds by the
heat of a wood-burning stove are
catcher Luke Sewell (left) and
pitcher Jimmy Zinn. This photo was
taken during spring training in New
Orleans on April 10, 1929.

1929 PARTIAL TEAM PHOTO. Numbers would first be worn on major league uniforms during the Indians' May 13 game at League Park against the Yankees.

Mr. and Mrs. Roger Peckinpaugh and Coach Grover Hartley on the Train, March 1929. Popular with the fans, Peckinpaugh was a former Cleveland sandlot player whose professional career peaked with the Yankees from 1913 to '21. Hartley had been a catcher for the Tribe in 1927.

Max Rosenblum Visits with Manager Roger Peckinpaugh, March 1929. Cleveland department store president Rosenblum, who ran a first-rate amateur baseball team, was also a co-founder of the American Basketball League, the country's first national professional basketball league (1925-31). The Cleveland franchise, called the Rosenblums, won the league title in 1929.

CLUBHOUSE MEETING IN JUNE 1933, PRESIDED OVER BY MANAGER WALTER JOHNSON.

TWO

The 1930s

The Bradley-Evans-Peckinpaugh regime continued into the 1930s, a period of mediocrity for the Indians. The team's highest win total in this decade was 87, achieved in 1932 and '39, and the closest they came to the pennant was the third-place finish of 1935, 12 games behind the Tigers. For the most part, fans had to content themselves with a thrilling game or two, a hot streak in April, or the efforts of individual players such as pitcher Wes Ferrell, who remained dominant in 1930 and '31 while the team was little better than average (81-73 and 78-76, respectively).

A fast start in 1930 raised hopes, but a precipitous skid in midsummer proved too much to overcome, even with an upturn in late August and early September, and the team finished 21 games out of first. Earl Averill hit .339 and, on September 17, smashed four home runs in one game against Washington. Second baseman Johnny Hodapp had a 22-game hitting streak while batting .354, and the .304 team batting average was notable; but the players' 237 errors undermined their own hitting. Similarly, in 1931 Averill hit 32 home runs (third best in the AL), but the team folded even sooner, slumping in May.

A much better 87-65 finish in 1932 was still good enough only for fourth place, 19 games out. The major event of the season was the first game in brand-new Cleveland Municipal Stadium on July 31, a 1–0 loss to Philadelphia which was attended by more than 80,000 people. It is worth mentioning here that the starting pitcher in that first game at the Stadium, Mel Harder, also threw out the first pitch in the *last* game there sixty-one years later! Although the colossal dimensions of the park (to which all remaining home games for that season were moved) were enhanced by a capacity crowd, a major problem quickly became apparent that would dog the ballclub for decades. With so many seats available, fans would never have difficulty obtaining tickets for anything other than Opening Day, an All-Star Game, or playoffs. As a result the crowds were often *smaller* than in the more intimate confines of League Park. The Stadium as originally configured was also a demoralizing park for power hitters, with the center field fence 470 feet away. No one in the history of Municipal Stadium ever did hit a ball into the centerfield bleachers, although in the 1950s the cannon-armed outfielder Rocky Colavito *threw* balls from home plate over the fence several times during workouts. For fifteen years, the Indians would waver with seeming indecision between the two ballparks.

In 1933 the Depression reached its worst point. Baseball felt the pinch, as each of the sixteen teams eliminated two roster spots, downgraded standards of travel, and reduced player salaries. The minor leagues were gutted. Attendance at the major-league level slacked off dramatically since fewer people could afford tickets. Players, fearful of sitting out and losing their already diminished contracts, played through injuries that would have sidelined them in any other era. Scheduled doubleheaders, promotional stunts, and (beginning in 1935 in some parks) night games under the lights were used to boost ticket sales.

Above all, the owners of major league clubs hoped to field winning teams, the best way to restore earnings. Manager Roger Peckinpaugh was popular with the media and fans, but owner Alva Bradley's patience with the Indians' slow progress was gone by June 1933, and he fired Peckinpaugh after a dismal East Coast swing. Former pitching great Walter Johnson was brought in to manage, but the team's play actually declined slightly over the rest of the season. Their final record was 75-76, attendance fell again, and General Manager Billy Evans' pay was also cut sharply. At the worst imaginable time, Bradley chose to discontinue the Tribe's radio broadcasts, in the belief that more people would be forced to come down to the park and buy tickets. Naturally, all that this accomplished was to further alienate the fans.

Home games were moved back to League Park in 1934 in an attempt to shore up attendance. A bad trade sent Wes Ferrell and Dick Porter to Boston and brought little except money in return (anticipating the trades of the cash-poor Gabe Paul era of the 1960s and 70s). Despite this the team improved to 85-69, but manager Johnson came under a great deal of criticism, and clashed with some of his players. An August slide put the team out of contention; Johnson, however, was re-signed.

The All-Star Game came to giant Municipal Stadium in 1935, but this was the only game played there during that season (the American League won 4–1). At League Park, things were not well with the Indians. A divisive rift arose between the players and the near-paranoid Walter Johnson. The fans grew hostile, and Bradley fired Johnson on August 4, replacing him with well-liked former Tribe catcher Steve O'Neill. Play picked up immediately and the team finished in third place at 82-71, with outfielder Joe Vosmik losing the AL batting title by a tiny margin on the final day of the season. GM Evans, feeling slighted by management, resigned on November 9th. A month later, pitcher Johnny Allen was acquired in a trade with the Yankees that would bear fruit two seasons later.

1936 was the year of one of the Indians' greatest finds, as new general manager C.C. "Cy" Slapnicka discovered a 16-year-old pitcher throwing rockets in sandlot ball in Van Meter, Iowa. Young Robert Feller was brought in for limited action in a July 6 exhibition game in Cleveland, and he struck out eight batters in short order. On September 13, pitching in a major-league game, Bob Feller struck out seventeen, breaking the AL record and tying Dizzy Dean's 1933 NL mark. First baseman Hal Trosky hit .343 with 162 RBI, and had a 28-game consecutive hitting streak. Several Tribe players went on hitting tears: Odell Hale hit safely in twenty-one straight games, and 20-game streaks were put up by Earl Averill, Roy Weatherly, and Joe Vosmik. The more relaxed atmosphere under Steve O'Neill did not translate to more wins, however, and the team's record slipped to 80-74, two and a half games worse than in 1935. A "June swoon" in the East ruined the 1937 campaign, and at season's end, with the final record a fourth-place 83-71, O'Neill was canned. On the bright side, pitcher Johnny Allen won fifteen straight games (17 straight dating back to the previous year), despite a substantial interruption for an appendectomy.

To replace the gentlemanly O'Neill, Tribe management made one of the worst managerial choices in its history by hiring Oscar Vitt. In the seasons to come, Vitt's behavior would precipitate greater friction with the players than had ever existed under Walter Johnson. The team played very well out of the gate in 1938 and stood in first place in June, but the Yankees passed them on July 13 and never looked back. Meanwhile, individual players had fine seasons, from outfielder Bruce Campbell's 27-game hitting streak to Bob Feller's 240 strikeouts, including a record-setting 18-KO game on the final day of the season in Municipal Stadium. The team finished in third place at 86-66, giving reason for optimism, but the players' relations with Vitt would begin to sour in 1939 when they wearied of his comments in the newspapers and his audible complaints behind their backs.

In June 1939, Earl Averill was unpopularly traded to Detroit by Cy Slapnicka for pitcher Harry Eisenstat. Two young players brought up in August from the minors, shortstop Lou Boudreau and second baseman Ray Mack, soon became a solid double-play combination, and Boudreau in particular would become one of the game's greatest players during the 1940s. Feller became a major star in '39, going 24-9 with a 2.85 ERA and 246 strikeouts. Nevertheless it was a streaky, roller coaster season which nearly duplicated the previous year's record at 87-57, and ended up with the club a distant twenty and a half games from the pennant. One notable 1939 "first" was the addition of seven night games under the lights.

At the end of the decade, there was little recent baseball excellence to look back upon in Cleveland. Things would not pick up immediately in the 1940s, but when they *did* pick up, it would be something to behold.

CARL LIND, ZEKE BONURA, AND EDDIE MORGAN IN NEW ORLEANS, MARCH 1930. "Banana Nose" Bonura (center) never played with the Indians in a regular-season game, but he made it to the show with the White Sox in 1934 and reached career highs in 1937, batting .345 with 100 RBI. He was a colorful and entertaining character who stole home to beat the Yankees in the 15th inning of a 1935 game, but he didn't endear himself to White Sox management with his contract holdouts, lax fielding, and especially his romantic interest in the daughter of owner J. Lou Comiskey. He was traded to the Senators before the season and finished his career with the Giants and Cubs.

A GREAT WASHINGTON NATIONALS BATTERY IS REUNITED IN KNOXVILLE, TENNESSEE. Pitcher Walter Johnson and catcher Eddie Ainsmith played together for Washington from 1910–1920. By the time of this April 1934 spring training photo, Johnson was in his first full season as the Indians' manager, while Ainsmith umpired in the Class A Southern Association. Two years later Johnson was elected to the Hall of Fame.

THE ST. LOUIS BROWNS' GREAT ROGERS HORNSBY WITH INDIANS GENERAL MANAGER BILLY EVANS, JUNE 1935. This was Evans' final season. Two events precipitated his departure: a rift with manager Walter Johnson in which Evans was not supported by owner Alva Bradley, and a draconian salary cut for which the Depression was given as justification. Evans was soon named farm director for the Red Sox. He was elected to the Hall of fame in 1973.

CENTER FIELDER EARL AVERILL SCORES AND IS CONGRATULATED BY FIRST BASEMAN HAL TROSKY IN MAY 1935. Averill, the only AL outfielder to play in the first six All-Star Games, had not reached the majors quickly. He joined the San Francisco Seals of the Pacific Coast League at age 24 after playing semipro baseball for several years. The Indians bought his contract and he hit .322 as a rookie in 1929, punctuating his arrival with a home run in his first at-bat. His finest seasons were in 1931 and '32, with a two-year record of 64 homers, 256 runs scored and 267 RBI. 1935 was a difficult year due to injuries, but Averill would storm back in 1936 to put up 232 hits while batting .378. In 1939, with his career in decline, he was traded to the Tigers. In 1965, a decade before Averill's election to the Hall of Fame, the Indians retired his jersey, No. 3.

FINAL PITCH OF A MASTERPIECE. On August 31, 1935, White Sox right-hander Lloyd Vernon Kennedy slips a called third strike past Indians left fielder Joe Vosmik, capping a 6–0 no-hitter.

27

THE GREAT LOU GEHRIG STRIKES OUT IN SEPTEMBER 1937, IN FRONT OF CATCHER FRANKIE PYTLAK. Getting Gehrig to swing and miss was an accomplishment. Tribe pitcher Mel Harder, who had an unusual degree of success against batters such as Ted Williams and Joe DiMaggio, struggled against Gehrig, who seemed to be able to hit anything thrown to him. Pytlak was a solid catcher with a .282 lifetime batting average as an Indian. In 125 games in 1937, he hit .315 with 125 hits.

INDIANS PITCHER WILLIS HUDLIN WITH NATE PEARSON OF THE YANKEES, JUNE 1937.
Hudlin's record of 12-11 in 1937 was almost exactly equivalent in winning percentage to the
83-71 season of the Tribe. A 2-11 Eastern swing was the centerpiece of a "June swoon," leading
to a fourth-place finish, nineteen games out.

WELCOMING A NEW SKIPPER IN DECEMBER 1937. From left to right are owner Alva Bradley,
newly-hired manager Oscar Vitt, and general manager Cy Slapnicka. Vitt, brought in to replace
the fired Steve O'Neill, became one of the most hated managers in the club's history.

ROY WEATHERLY AND HAL TROSKY, MAY 1938. As a rookie in 1934, Trosky (right) had established himself with statistics comparable to those of Yankee first baseman Lou Gehrig—35 HR, 142 RBI and a .330 average. In 1936 he hit .343 with 42 homers and a team-record 162 RBI, part of a run of six consecutive seasons with 100 or more RBI. His self-imposed pressure to play well led to a troublesome series of migraine headaches, which forced his retirement in 1941 (and disqualified him from military service).

EARL AVERILL HITTING IN THE 1930s.

Detroit First Baseman Hank Greenberg Singles in October 1938. Ten years before Jackie Robinson became the first African-American major leaguer with the Brooklyn Dodgers, four-time All-Star Greenberg was baseball's first great Jewish player. In twelve seasons with Detroit and one with Pittsburgh from 1930–47, Hammerin' Hank hit the ball at a .313 clip with 331 career home runs, and *averaged* an astonishing 148 RBIs (with a peak of 183 RBI in 1937). He won the American League MVP award in 1935 and '40 and was enshrined in Cooperstown in 1956. He also served with distinction in World War II. He was a favorite of Cleveland owner Bill Veeck, who hired him in 1948 as farm system director and promoted him to general manager in 1950, and later brought him to the White Sox.

Chief Wheelock of the Oneida Tribe Wishes Manager Oscar Vitt Luck on Opening Day 1938.

PELICAN PARK, NEW ORLEANS, IN 1939. New Orleans was the Indians' spring training location in 1902-03, 1905-06, 1912, 1916-20, and 1928-29. The Pelicans were a minor-league team that played in this stadium in two separate locations. Pelican Park (or Stadium) was originally located at Banks Street and South Carrollton Avenue. In 1914-15 the ballpark was disassembled and moved down Carrollton by mules to the intersection with Tulane Avenue, where it was reopened on April 13, 1915. The final game before the park's demolition was played on Sunday, September 1, 1957.

A STUDY IN CONTRAST. Outfielder Roy Weatherly (5'6") and pitcher Mike Naymick (6'8") each sacrificed two years of baseball to serve in the military. "Stormy" Weatherly, who played for Cleveland from 1936 to '42, was regarded as a bit of a complainer by AL umpires. He got off to a strong start as a rookie, hitting in twenty consecutive games. Weatherly was traded to the Yankees after the 1942 season and served in the military from 1942 to '44, returning for two more seasons. Naymick, who went into the military in 1941, pitched sparingly for the Tribe in the two seasons before and the two after his tour of duty, with but a 5-7 record in fifty-one appearances.

OPENING DAY 1939. As the Indians prepare to take on the Detroit Tigers, Judy Garland (at microphone) sings the National Anthem at Municipal Stadium.

JOE DIMAGGIO AND JOE GALLAGHER WATCH FROM THE YANKEES' DUGOUT DURING A 1939 GAME. The great Yankee Clipper had a terrible time batting against longtime Tribe hurler Mel Harder, who liked to throw the sinkerball (DiMaggio's weakness). DiMaggio batted only .180 lifetime against Harder.

GAME ACTION AT LEAGUE PARK, SEPTEMBER 1939. The ballpark at E. 66th and Lexington was built in 1890 by the ownership of the old Cleveland Spiders. A decade later the Cleveland American League club negotiated a rental agreement to play its games in the ballpark. The intersection there of two trolley lines made going to the game by streetcar convenient for both fans and players. League Park would be the Tribe's sole home until its first game at the cavernous new Municipal Stadium on July 31, 1932. Similar to Jacobs Field in terms of intimacy and closeness to the action, League Park with its short fences was enjoyed by hitters but not pitchers. The new downtown Stadium was the largest in baseball, but fans would also quickly catch on to the fact that there was little urgency to buy tickets, since seats were almost always available.

CLEVELAND MUNICIPAL STADIUM IN 1938. After 107 games at the Stadium with less-than-expected attendance, the team returned to League Park for the entire seasons of 1934 and 1935 (except for the '35 All-Star Game), and all but one game in 1936. Gradually thereafter Municipal Stadium became home to the Indians, who played fifteen games there in 1937, 18 in 1938, 30 (including the American League's first night game) in 1939, 49 in 1940, and 32 in 1941. Over the next four years the club went to the Stadium for forty-odd games each season, saying farewell to League Park with a final game there on September 21, 1946. Interestingly, while one crumbling part of the old League Park grandstand still survives today alongside a recreational ballfield, after Jacobs Field opened in 1994 the remains of the Stadium were pushed into Lake Erie to serve as a fish reef and to make way for the construction of Cleveland Browns Stadium, which opened in 1999.

AN EXCITED CROWD ARRIVES FOR A WORLD SERIES GAME IN 1948.

THREE

The 1940s

For the Indians, the decade of the 1940s began with a bang. Bob Feller took the mound at Cleveland Stadium on the first day of the 1940 season and blanked the White Sox 1–0 in what remains the only Opening Day no-hitter ever pitched in the big leagues. It was the first sign of an utterly dominant season for Feller, who showed astonishing durability in pitching 31 complete games and a total of 320 1/3 innings, amassing a 27-11 record with 261 strikeouts and a 2.61 ERA.

The rest of the summer of 1940 was exciting, too, as the Tribe won 89 games and stayed strongly in contention until the pennant-winning Tigers eliminated them three days before the end of the season. Some of the players' competitiveness had been eroded by their fractious relations with manager Oscar Vitt, who was fired after the season. Improbably, Roger Peckinpaugh was rehired as manager, more than seven years after being fired. The roster was shuffled and rookies were tried, and the 1941 season got off to a fast start until the team hit the skids in July. There was some excitement amid the slide, though, as Joe DiMaggio brought his record consecutive-game hitting streak (which had begun on May 15) to Cleveland Stadium. On July 17, with the streak at 56 games, 67,468 fans jammed the Stadium to see if DiMaggio could keep it going. The Indians saw to it that he didn't.

Another brilliant campaign from Feller couldn't save a 75-79 team. At the end of the 1941 season Peckinpaugh was booted upstairs to replace Cy Slapnicka, who had resigned as GM due to illness. After reading about the managerial vacancy in the newspaper, twenty-four-year-old shortstop Lou Boudreau wrote a letter to Alva Bradley, offering to serve as player-manager in 1942. Boudreau was brought in to meet the team's directors, and after lengthy debate he was installed as manager—in part because of the marketing appeal.

But baseball, along with everything else, would be changed on December 7th when Japan attacked Pearl Harbor and America was drawn into the war. Many of major league baseball's best players would either serve in the military or work in war-related industries, and replacements, retreads and second-raters (many of them with physical military deferments) tried their best to fill the gaps. Boudreau was learning how to manage, and the results were mixed at first. In 1942, with Feller serving in the Navy and Hal Trosky forced into retirement with migraines, the Indians put up a second consecutive 75-79 season. New governmental travel restrictions in 1943 led the team to begin three years of "spring" training at Purdue University in sunny West Lafayette, Indiana. The '43 Indians season got off to a strong start, but the slump the team fell into in June went on too long to be salvaged by a revival in August, and Boudreau had to settle for 82 wins and third place. In 1944 the Tribe stayed in the race until a September slide dropped them like a stone and led to a 72-82 finish, but Boudreau won the AL batting title at .327 (needing, and getting, a hit in his final at-bat to do so).

In 1945 Ken Keltner joined the Navy and Ray Mack the Army, and Mel Harder worked half the season in a war-related industry. The Indians bounced back and forth between League Park and Municipal Stadium, never really feeling at home anywhere, and finished a half-game over .500. Bob Feller returned in late August after losing more than three seasons in the Navy, and pitched like he'd never been away. The mass return of veterans to the major leagues occurred in the '46 season, a forgettable 68-86 campaign for Cleveland. Most of the Indians except for Feller had a bad year, but more important events were taking place that would change the team's fortunes for the better. A war veteran and savvy baseball marketer named Bill Veeck bought the Indians on June 22. He immediately set about restoring some luster to the faded franchise, resuming radio broadcasts of the games (with Jack Graney and Bob Neal) less than a week into his tenure, taking over the general manager responsibilities from the departed Peckinpaugh, and doing anything he could to increase ticket sales through entertaining and often bizarre promotions. Veeck shook up the roster after the season, sending pitcher Allie Reynolds to the Yankees in an October trade which brought second baseman Joe Gordon, dealing again with New York in December to get knuckleballer Gene Bearden and outfielder Hal Peck, and sending outfielder Gene Woodling to the Pirates for catcher Al Lopez. Navy veteran Bob Lemon, a rookie outfielder with a strong arm, was tried at pitcher, and would join the staff permanently in the following season. Veeck also determined that, starting in 1947, all home games would be played at Municipal Stadium.

The team improved to a fourth-place 80-74 record in 1947, but Veeck wasn't satisfied. Players came and went as if in a revolving door. Seeking to make the Stadium more hitter-friendly, the ebullient Veeck had a new interior fence installed which shortened the power alleys and center field, and he even secretly moved the fence from day to day according to the pitching and hitting match-ups, until this was declared illegal the following season. But the most attention was commanded by his midseason signing of Larry Doby, a star in the Negro National League and the second African-American to join the major leagues.

Doby played in his first Indians game on July 5, eleven weeks after Jackie Robinson's debut in the National League. Brought in as an infielder without any clear roster spot to fill, he made comparatively little impact in his first half-season. In 1948 he was able (as Robinson had been with the Dodgers a year previously) to go through spring training and become comfortable with the club, and at the same time he was learning under Tris Speaker's guidance to play in center field, where the Indians could better use him.

Everything came together for the Cleveland Indians in the magical year of 1948, although not everything was in place from the beginning. The fielding and hitting were generally outstanding, but in midseason Veeck realized that he needed another quality pitcher. He rolled the dice by signing legendary Negro Leagues pitcher Satchel Paige, after staging a tryout to convince a skeptical Lou Boudreau that the venerable Satch could still pitch. The gamble paid off handsomely as a fired-up Paige contributed significantly to the Indians' pennant drive down the stretch. Jimmy Dudley, who joined Jack Graney in the radio booth in 1948, would become an institution in the years to come.

A nail-biter pennant race culminated in the single most significant game in American League history, the one-game playoff against the Red Sox in Fenway Park on October 4, famously won by Gene Bearden, who pitched a complete game on two days' rest (and by the bat of Boudreau, who was selected as the league's MVP). The World Series against the Boston Braves is often spoken of as "anticlimactic," but who can imagine such a thing in championship-hungry Cleveland?

The Indians took the Series four games to two as centerfielder Larry Doby justified Veeck's confidence, batting .318 with seven hits and two RBI. There was one bittersweet footnote to the championship. Thirteen-year veteran Bob Feller was brilliant in Game One, allowing just two hits, but Boston's Johnny Sain threw a 1–0 shutout to defeat him. Feller would not come as close in Game 5, losing 11–5, and never would get the World Series victory he deserved. Cleveland pitcher Steve Gromek outlasted Sain 2–1 in a nerve-wracking Game 4. Gene Bearden, who got a shutout victory in Game 3, entered as a reliever in Game 6 and preserved the win for Bob Lemon. The Indians were World Champions for the second time in their history.

Veeck made a brilliant deal for future pitching in December 1948, acquiring right-hander Early Wynn along with first baseman Mickey Vernon from Washington. But the decade ended on a letdown. As brilliant as Veeck had been in facilitating his team's success leading up to the championship, his efforts to capitalize on every last bit of marketing potential may have undermined the players in 1949. Day after day during homestands, they had morning calls for the shooting of a baseball film with which Veeck was involved, but the lack of rest and time away from the park increased their fatigue. Age and injuries were catching up with the team, and they struggled to a third-place 89-65 finish. On September 24th, with the Indians eliminated from the race, Veeck staged a parody funeral for the 1948 pennant. When he sold the team on November 22, a brief and lively era came to an end, but a decade of exciting, competitive baseball was ahead.

OPENING DAY MILESTONE. Bob Feller pitched the only opening day no-hitter in major league history against the White Sox in Comiskey Park on Tuesday, April 16, 1940. Assembling for a happy postgame photo are starting catcher Rollie Hemsley (left), manager Oscar Vitt, and Feller. Vitt was not always so gracious behind Feller's back. Audible grumbling by the manager while Feller was on the mound was one of many missteps which turned the players against Vitt, eventually leading to near-mutiny and, finally, to Vitt's firing after the 1941 season.

GETTING IN SHAPE FOR OPENING DAY 1941. Pictured from left to right are Richard Klein, Jim Hegan, Dewey Adkins, and Donald Pulford. Only Hegan would play for the Tribe, although pitcher Adkins did see brief action (a total of sixteen innings) in 1942 and 1943 with Washington. In his third and final major league season he pitched 82 innings for the 1949 Cubs, going 2-4 with a 5.68 ERA.

THREE LEGENDS OF THE GAME, CLEVELAND AMATEUR DAY, JULY 1941. Pictured from left to right are Ty Cobb, Babe Ruth, and Tris Speaker.

OSCAR MELILLO AND BURT
SHOTTEN, LOU BOUDREAU'S 1942
COACHES.

OUTFIELDER ORIS HOCKETT IS
CONGRATULATED BY KEN KELTNER
AFTER GETTING A HOME RUN
AGAINST THE PHILADELPHIA A'S AT
LEAGUE PARK IN JUNE 1942. Third
baseman Keltner, whose greatest
claim to fame was making two
difficult plays in foul territory to stop
Joe DiMaggio's hitting streak at 56
games in 1941, was one of the best
infielders of his era.

COMMISSIONER KENESAW MOUNTAIN LANDIS CHATS WITH INDIANS OWNER ALVA BRADLEY. The occasion was the opening of the major leagues' Post-War Planning Committee sessions, which took place in February 1944.

MICKEY ROCCO HITS A TRIPLE IN AUGUST 1944. With several of the Indians' star players serving in the armed forces during World War II, Rocco was one of the players who filled in, playing at first base and hitting .258 from 1943 to '46. The catcher is Hal Wagner, traded to the Red Sox earlier that season by the Philadelphia Athletics.

SPRING TRAINING 1945. Pictured from left to right are Pitcher Erv Palica, pitcher Ed Klieman, catcher Hank Ruzkowski, pitcher Bill Bonness, and Pat Leevey (seated). Only Klieman, Ruzkowski and Bonness would make the team, but Palica (a converted shortstop) broke through with Brooklyn in 1945 and went 41-55 over a ten-year career with the Dodgers and Orioles.

LOU BOUDREAU AND UTILITY INFIELDER AL CIHOCKI, 1945. In his only season in the majors, Cihocki (right) batted .219 in 92 games. Boudreau, in contrast, was one of the most renowned players in the history of the Indians. A slick-fielding shortstop with a potent bat, Boudreau also capitalized on a managerial vacuum after the 1941 season. Just 24 years old, he managed to convince Tribe management that he could be an effective skipper, and thus began the nine-year reign of the "Boy Manager." It would all culminate in the magical 1948 season, when Boudreau won the American League MVP Award while managing the Indians to the World Championship.

CATCHER SHERM LOLLAR, LOU BOUDREAU, PITCHER BOB LEMON, FIRST BASEMAN EDDIE
ROBINSON, LATE APRIL 1946. Lollar (left) would stay only one season with the Indians, but
played on for seventeen more years, averaging .264 and 75 RBI over a solid career with the
Yankees, St. Louis Browns, and White Sox.

PITCHER ALLIE REYNOLDS GREETS VISITING INDIANS FROM CANADA IN MAY 1946.
Reynolds, himself a Native American, was called "Super Chief" by teammates. An extremely
hard thrower who had difficulty consistently getting the ball over for strikes during his four full
seasons with the Indians, Reynolds fulfilled his great potential only after being traded to the
Yankees before the 1947 season.

BILL VEECK (LEFT), LOU BOUDREAU, AND BOB FELLER IN JUNE 1946. Feller struck out 348 batters during this season, en route to a 26-15 record, all the more amazing since he had not pitched for almost four years while serving in the Navy. Discovered by GM Cy Slapnicka as a sixteen-year old in Iowa, Feller came up to the majors in 1936 and more than lived up to his billing, throwing a wicked fastball and establishing a legendary reputation for craftiness, durability and competitiveness. He pitched at top form well into the 1950s, ending his career as part of the Big Four starting pitching staff with Bob Lemon, Mike Garcia and Early Wynn. The Indians retired his jersey, No. 19, in 1957, and he was elected to the Hall of Fame in 1962.

BILL VEECK ON CLEVELAND'S FIRST LADIES' DAY, JULY 1946. This was the revival of a tradition which Veeck's father had instituted as president of the Chicago Cubs. Women paid only a service charge instead of full ticket price.

RIGHT FIELDER HANK EDWARDS HOMERS IN JULY 1946. Edwards, a solid young player who progressed quickly during his first two full seasons, 1942 and '43, set aside his career (like many other players) to serve in the war. Upon returning to baseball in 1946, he picked up where he had left off by hitting .301, but a serious shoulder injury two years later shortened his time in the major leagues. In this photo he is met at the plate by Heinz Becker, a former minor-leaguer with Bill Veeck's Milwaukee franchise, who played in only 52 games at first base for the Tribe.

CATCHER JIM HEGAN, DOWN BUT NOT OUT. Hegan, a relatively light hitter, was known as the best defensive catcher and signal-caller of his era. His toughness was also evident during this August 1946 contest as, hit hard in the chest by a pitched ball, he shook it off and finished the game.

PIONEER LARRY DOBY IN 1947. One of only five Indians players to have their numbers retired, Hall of Famer Doby has long been thought of as "the American League's Jackie Robinson." Though he was signed by the Tribe eleven weeks after the Dodgers legend made his NL debut, Doby may have suffered a more difficult transition. Robinson had the benefit of going through spring training, whereas Doby was brought in cold during the season, with no room for him in the infield where the lineup was set. At first the reaction of many of his white teammates was uncertain or even standoffish (in part, perhaps, because it wasn't clear where he could help the club), but Joe Gordon and others befriended him. He was met with hostility from certain players around the league, but before long, Indians pitchers were throwing at opponents who insulted him.

PLAYER/MANAGER LOU BOUDREAU, WITH GEORGE KELL OF THE TIGERS, OCTOBER 1947.
Owner Bill Veeck, who liked Boudreau and was awed by his play at shortstop, was not sold on
his managerial ability. Around the time that this photo was taken, Veeck was secretly
attempting to work out a deal to trade Boudreau to the St. Louis Browns. The Browns finally
said no, but Veeck managed to turn it into a marketing bonus. The pondered trade was leaked
to the newspapers as if it was still alive, and then was "canceled" after a public outcry. Veeck
came out looking as if he had gracefully bowed to the will of the fans.

OUTFIELDER DALE MITCHELL. A dependable batter with a career .312 average, Mitchell had four
hitting streaks of more than twenty consecutive games during his eleven years with the Indians. In
this photo, Mitchell slides into second on Hal Peck's single on the last day of the 1947 season, a 1–0
Tigers victory over Bob Feller and the Tribe. The helpful arrow was added by the *Cleveland Press.*

48

CHAMPIONSHIP-CALIBER HUSTLE. New Tribe centerfielder Thurman Tucker slides by the St. Louis Browns' Bob Dillinger into third base, after stealing second and reaching third on a throw which was bobbled by second baseman Jerry Priddy. Bob Feller threw a two-hitter in this Indians victory in April 1948. As the season progressed, Tucker lost his starting job but remained a dependable role player. He would make two tough, crucial plays in Game 6 of the World Series, in which the Tribe won the World Championship. Tucker remained with the club as a utilityman until 1951.

THE BEST STARTING INFIELD EVER? Pictured from left to right are Third baseman Ken Keltner, shortstop Lou Boudreau, second baseman Joe Gordon, and first baseman Eddie Robinson, in a photo from spring training, 1948.

NEW OWNER BILL VEECK WITH STARLET ANN BLYTH, 1946.
Raising money in very creative ways, Veeck bought the Indians out from under Alva Bradley's group, and blew into Cleveland like a hurricane. He immediately set about remaking the team in a number of ingenious and fan-friendly ways, which included circus-like promotions, Ladies' Days, "tribute" nights, and morning games for the enjoyment of night-shift workers. Attendance soared immediately as Veeck made the ballpark a fun place to visit again. His fair and respectful treatment of players also went a long way toward creating a happy clubhouse.

BILL VEECK WATCHES SATCHEL PAIGE'S FAMOUS TRYOUT IN 1948.
Aware that the Indians' pitching staff was not deep enough to get the team over the hump in a difficult pennant race, Veeck decided to bring the forty-something Paige in to throw for manager Lou Boudreau on July 7. The audition consisted of Paige pitching for twenty minutes to Boudreau, who first caught and then batted. Locating each pitch impeccably, Paige quickly won over the skeptical Boudreau (who had previously heard that Paige's fastball had faded). Once hired, the longtime Negro leagues superstar more than lived up to the promise shown in this session, going 6-1 with a 2.48 ERA over the rest of the season.

SATCHEL PAIGE GIVES ADVICE TO OLYMPIC FOUR-TIME GOLD MEDALIST HARRISON DILLARD. Cleveland native Dillard, who was at Municipal Stadium to receive an award before this 1948 game, is the only man ever to win Olympic gold medals in both the sprints and high hurdles. A graduate of East Tech High School, Dillard built on the legend of East Tech's Jesse Owens in racing to Olympic track and field glory in 1948 and 1952. While at Baldwin-Wallace College, he won four national collegiate titles and fourteen AAU outdoor titles in the high and low hurdles. He later had a successful career in public relations.

PAIGE AT BAT AGAINST THE WASHINGTON NATIONALS, AUGUST 1948. Although he contributed very little as a batter in his few years in the major leagues, the rangy Satch had an inimitable stance at the plate. Off the field Paige led an entertaining and unpredictable life, but at the ballpark he was a tough competitor and a dedicated teammate. He got his plaque in Cooperstown in 1971.

DON BLACK SUFFERS A BRAIN HEMORRHAGE ON SEPTEMBER 13, 1948. Trainer Lefty Weisman (left) and Coach Bill McKechnie attend to the pitcher, who collapsed while he was batting. Removed from this game against the St. Louis Browns, Black was rushed to the hospital and miraculously survived the aneurism without surgery, but he never played again. Owner Bill Veeck later staged a benefit to help with Black's medical costs.

A DISPUTED CALL IN LATE SEPTEMBER 1948, AS THE PENNANT RACE NARROWS. Pictured from left to right are Bob Lemon, Ed Robinson, Joe Gordon, Lou Boudreau, umpire Bill McKinley, and Jim Hegan. There had been a riveting four-team race for much of the season, but in September the Yankees and the Philadelphia Athletics faded, leaving the Indians and the Boston Red Sox to battle it out. The teams drew even on the last day of the season, setting up a one-game playoff at Fenway Park which is now part of legend.

A Pennant-winner on One Day's Rest. Winning pitcher Gene Bearden is carried off the field after beating the Red Sox in the famous playoff game in 1948, just two days after he pitched a game against Detroit. Player-Manager Lou Boudreau's risky decision to start the knuckleballer, implemented after consultation with the rest of the players in a clubhouse meeting, proved to be an inspired one.

BOSTON SKIPPER JOE MCCARTHY CONGRATULATES LOU BOUDREAU AFTER THE HISTORIC ONE-GAME PLAYOFF. In the Indians' 8–3 victory in the AL playoff game, Oct. 4, 1948, Boudreau contributed mightily, going 4-for-4 with 2 home runs.

CLEVELAND FANS LINE UP FOR SERIES TICKETS, OCTOBER 1948.

An Unusual Fielding Technique. First baseman Eddie Robinson, with the ball, slides into the bag to beat the Braves' Alvin Dark (a future Tribe manager) on a grounder in the 1st inning of Game One of the 1948 Series. The umpire is Bill Summers.

Harpo Marx "Clowns It Up" with Outfielder Gus Zernial and Ladies during Pre-game Ceremonies in Early April, 1947.

THE INDIANS WALK OFF THE FIELD AFTER WINNING THE 1948 WORLD SERIES.

1948 VICTORY PARADE: BOUDREAU AND VEECK. Despite his longtime doubts about whether Boudreau's brilliance as a shortstop was matched by his managerial ability, Veeck was more than happy to toast the Boy Manager on this night. Both have plaques in the Hall of Fame today.

CLEVELAND FANS CELEBRATE WITH THE PRESS.

UTILITY INFIELDER JOHNNY BERARDINO AFTER BEING HIT BY A PITCH, AUGUST 1949. Berardino (second from right), while not a star, was a very capable fielder and role player, and a member of the Championship team of 1948. In years to come, his fame would greatly exceed that of any of his Indians teammates. An actor since childhood, Berardino (who later removed the second "r" from his last name) landed the role of Dr. Steve Hardy on "General Hospital," and played the character for decades.

EXTRA-INNINGS HERO. Catcher Jim Hegan is congratulated by pitcher Al Benton after a 14th-inning homer that won a game in late August, 1949. This was one of the highlights in an otherwise disappointing year. The Indians overcame a terrible first two months of the season to finish in third place at 89-65.

MOCK FUNERAL FOR LAST SEASON'S CHAMPIONSHIP PENNANT, SEPTEMBER 24, 1949. After the Indians have been eliminated from contention, team president Rudie Schaffer reads aloud from *The Sporting News* while Veeck "chokes up." The 1948 pennant was buried behind the centerfield fence.

THE BIG FOUR: PITCHERS EARLY WYNN, MIKE GARCIA, BOB LEMON AND BOB FELLER, 1953. A look at the won-lost record of these four in 761 starts from 1949 through 1955 illustrates their dominance, comparable to that of any pitching staff in any era. Over this stretch of time Feller was 89-60, Garcia 115-70, Lemon 146-78, and Wynn 129-74, for a combined record of 479-282 (.629 winning percentage). Feller, a few years older than the others, was 0-4 and past his prime by 1956, but if the young Herb Score (20-9) is substituted for Feller, the "new" Big Four still turned in a 71-44 (.617) record in '56. Unfortunately, Score's brilliance would be cut short in 1957.

FOUR
The 1950s

The Yankees owned the Fifties. The Bronx Bombers claimed every American League pennant in the decade except for 1954 and 1959, and they won the World Series six times. The Indians were a strong team during most of those years, but their best efforts always fell just a little short—except for one glorious season. Still, the Tribe was a fun team to watch, and through the 1956 season their great pitchers usually kept them in a game.

The Indians got off to a bad start in 1950 as the pitching uncharacteristically sputtered, but the team's play picked up and they remained in contention until September. New GM Hank Greenberg—who had long shared the departed Bill Veeck's doubts about Lou Boudreau's managerial ability—made many personnel changes, including selling the contract of '48 playoff hero Gene Bearden (who had gone 8-8 in 1949 and never returned to form). The infield received a makeover, with Al Rosen now at third, Ray Boone at shortstop (and Boudreau relegated to utility status), Bobby Avila at second, and eventually Luke Easter—who launched a McGwire-esque 477-foot blast into the upper deck on June 23—at first. 92 wins in 1950 were good enough only for fourth place, however, and Greenberg fired Boudreau on November 10th.

A questionable trade early in the 1951 season sent the young and talented outfielder Minnie Minoso to the White Sox, where he would spend the best years of his career before returning to Cleveland in 1957. New manager Al Lopez guided the team to exactly one more victory than in Boudreau's final season. Bob Feller returned to greatness, going 22-8 over 249 2/3 innings and throwing his third career no-hitter on July 1st. Dale Mitchell hit safely in 23 consecutive games, Larry Doby put up a 21-game streak, and the season too was streaky, starting well but roller coasting through periods of winning and losing. The Tribe lost its grip on first place on September 15th, quickly sliding out of contention afterwards.

With Feller registering a subpar 9-13 record and the defense often suspect, 1952 was another up-and-down season, and for the second year in a row the Tribe finished in second place at 93-61. The Yankees proved to be uncatchable at the end of the season, despite a terrific finish in which the Indians won 24 of their last 33 games. Frustration began to mount and attendance fell sharply for the second straight year in 1953 as the team slipped to 92 victories and turned in yet another second-place effort. (How the fans of the 1970s or 1980s would have welcomed even *one* second-place finish!) Just as in 1952, a season-ending hot streak came too late to get the Indians over the hump.

It all changed in 1954. Left-handed pitcher Hal Newhouser was signed as a free agent on April 12, and Vic Wertz, acquired in a June 1st trade with the Orioles, took over for Luke Easter (who had bad knees) at first base. The Big Four pitchers, along with fellow starter Art Houtemann, rolled over the opposition with a record of 93-36. A combined 228 RBI from Larry Doby and Al Rosen, and Bobby Avila's AL-best .341 batting average, supported the spectacular pitching. After a rough start, the Tribe caught fire and climbed to first place in mid-May. An additional highlight was the All-Star Game at Cleveland Stadium in July, in which the American League triumphed 11-9. In August, mowing down the rest of the league, the team defined what was becoming a year of greatness. Although New York remained in contention until the final week, the Indians finally threw off the Yankees' domination in an epic 111-43 season which surpassed the 1927 Yankees' record by one game.

That was the good news.

The bad news was the World Series against the New York Giants. Willie Mays' astonishing running catch and throw on Vic Wertz's 460-foot fly ball to center in Game One at the Polo Grounds has become the symbol of the surprising four-game sweep (in four quick days) by the Giants, which crushed the spirits of Tribe fans. The hitting of Dusty Rhodes and the fine pitching from Johnny Antonelli and Preston Gomez actually did more damage than Mays' catch. The Cleveland offense slumbered until Hank Majewski's three-run homer in Game 4, which was too little and too late. It would be the Indians' last World Series appearance for 41 years.

In 1955 the Tribe matched its 93-61 records from 1951 and '52, and Cleveland had a second-place team once again. Through May the Indians seemed destined to hang tough as they had done in 1954, but they were inconsistent over the rest of the season, ended with a slump, and watched the Yankees power past them. The pitching had declined somewhat from the previous season, but hard-throwing lefty Herb Score came up from the minors and dazzled everyone, winning the AL Rookie of the Year Award and establishing himself as the heir apparent to Bob Feller. The guard was changing, and after the season Larry Doby was traded to the White Sox for two unmemorable players. Second place was again the Indians' destination in 1956, but a more distant second. The team looked good through mid-May, just as one year earlier, but could not keep up the pace and slipped to an 88-66 record, precipitating the resignation of worn-out manager Al Lopez. Two young phenoms were turning heads: in 101 games, outfielder Rocky Colavito hit .276 with 21 home runs, and his buddy Herb Score was a sensation, going 20-9.

All good things must come to an end, sometimes prematurely. Score's 1957 season ended early and abruptly when he was hit in the eye by a line drive from the Yankees' Gil McDougald. Many believe that his career was ruined on that night; in any case, he would never again be the pitcher he was before the accident. The Big Four as a unit were history, and there was a lack of depth on the '57 pitching staff even before the loss of Score. Despite Colavito's 25 homers, 116 hits and 84 RBI, it was a year of ill omen for the Indians. Under new manager Kerby Farrell, the team finished one game under .500, the first losing season in a decade, and attendance fell steeply. Ferrell was fired by GM Hank Greenberg after the season, and then Greenberg himself was pink-slipped. The stage was set for the arrival of the Tribe's own "Darth Trader," a man whose name older Cleveland sports fans still curse: Frank Lane.

Over the next few seasons Lane would make an astonishing number of deals, often inexplicable if not downright idiotic, and he relished the daily headlines which his transactions brought. He got out of the gate quickly, trading Big Four pitcher Early Wynn and outfielder Al Smith to the White Sox for Minnie Minoso (a fine but aging player) and third baseman Fred Hatfield on December 4, 1957. The trade of Wynn was a shot across the bow, signaling that no player was sacred; and worse was to come. On February 18, catcher Jim Hegan and pitcher Hank Aguirre were sent to Detroit for two unknowns, and in June, *Lane traded away Roger Maris!* Maris and two others brought only Woodie Held and Vic Power in return; they were good players (Power won four straight Gold Gloves) but they didn't hit 61 homers in 1961 like Maris did. During the 1958 season the pitching staff was plagued by injuries, and the performance on the field improved by only one game, to 77-76. Attendance declined further, to the lowest levels since the end of the war, as the fans registered their disapproval with the poor play and with trading for trading's sake. New manager Bobby Bragan was fired by Lane on June 26 and replaced by former Tribe second baseman Joe Gordon. On August 23 Lane, angry over a single wild pitch, sold the contract of the expert knuckleballer Hoyt Wilhelm to Baltimore. Rocky Colavito had come of age as a major star and local hero in 1958, batting .303 with 41 homers, 148 hits and 113 RBI, but he would be subjected to contract lowballing and trade rumors instigated by Lane.

1959 was the Last Fling. A good trade, for once, sent the recently reacquired Larry Doby to Detroit for outfielder-first baseman Tito Francona, who would punch out 125 hits and 20 home runs with a .363 average, to go along with the 111 RBI and 42 homers by Colavito (who hit four homers in one game against Baltimore on July 10). Minoso won a Gold Glove in the outfield. The team started very well and led the league at the All-Star break, but they saw their chances slip away during a four-game sweep by Chicago at the end of August. A struggling Herb Score won no games after the All-Star break. The Indians finished the season with an 89-65 record and watched the White Sox, now owned by Bill Veeck and skippered by Al Lopez, win the AL pennant. Lane's second-guessing and undermining of Gordon led to tension and distraction, and at the end of the season the manager was fired and suddenly rehired.

No one knew it, but the Good Old Days were over, and the abyss lay just ahead.

LOU BOUDREAU AND ACTRESS SHELLEY WINTERS IN 1950. While enjoying himself here, Boudreau would enjoy the season to a lesser degree. Ninety-two wins would be enough only for fourth place, and first-year GM Hank Greenberg would fire Boudreau after the season.

FIRST BASEMAN LUKE EASTER, SHORTSTOP RAY BOONE, BOB FELLER, JIM HEGAN IN 1950. Taking over for the departed Lou Boudreau, with whom he had platooned in 1949, Boone (second from left) had his best Indians season, hitting .301 with 58 RBI— slightly better stats than Boudreau's in 1949 but a far cry from the .355/106 RBI season had by the player-manager in 1948.

LARRY DOBY HITS A HOME RUN IN 1950. This was a fine season for Doby, who hit .326 with 102 RBI, and started in the All-Star Game (one of six straight appearances from 1949 to '54). Once he established himself as a center fielder by learning the position in spring training of 1948, Doby became the star player that Bill Veeck had predicted he would become when he had first introduced Doby to the team.

SHORTSTOP RAY BOONE MAKES CONTACT, 1952. His career blossomed after he was traded to Detroit in 1953 and then switched to third base. Boone, along with his son Bob and grandsons Bret and Aaron, have forged a family baseball dynasty.

LARRY DOBY IS SAFE
AGAINST THE ST. LOUIS
BROWNS IN AN AUGUST
1950 GAME. Pitcher Don
Johnson covers first, and
Oscar Melillo is the first base
coach.

OUTFIELDER JIM FRIDLEY WITH PITCHER BOB LEMON AND LARRY DOBY IN JUNE 1952. The
little-known Fridley (left) played for the Indians only in 1952, hitting .251 but with little power
and few RBIs.

THIRD BASEMAN AL ROSEN IN 1952. Few have had as far-ranging and successful a tenure in baseball as Rosen, who during the latter half of his career served as president of the Yankees, the Houston Astros, and the San Francisco Giants. He first distinguished himself as a rookie with the Indians in 1950 (after three seasons in which he came up briefly from the minors) by winning the AL home run title with 37 (a league rookie record) and driving in 116 runs. His production remained high over the next two seasons, but his best year was 1953 when he won a unanimous American League MVP Award with 43 homers and 145 RBI. In 1954 Rosen was the All-Star Game MVP with two homers. He was a team leader during the pennant drive that year, battling through despite an injured finger which greatly compromised his swing and power.

EARLY WYNN AND LUKE EASTER AFTER A 1952 VICTORY. Easter, a former Negro leagues star, had to wait until age 34 to join the major leagues, but he made up for lost time when he got there. In 1952 he dueled with Larry Doby for the AL home run title, getting 31 to Doby's 32. His 477-foot homer in 1951 is the longest ever recorded at Municipal Stadium. The Indians family was shaken in 1979 when Easter, working as a bank messenger, was shot to death during a robbery.

TWENTY WINS APIECE AND COUNTING IN 1952. Pitchers Mike Garcia (left) and Early Wynn hold up all of their fingers to indicate the number of wins had by each. Garcia reached 20 on September 9, Wynn on the 11th (the day on which this photo was taken), during a series against the Philadelphia A's. Wynn's final record was 23-12, Garcia's 22-11.

THE YOUNG PHENOM. Outfielder Rocky Colavito writes his first letter home from spring training in February 1953 as GM Hank Greenberg looks on. Colavito more than lived up to his promise, making the big league club in 1956 and hitting 21, 25, 41 and 42 homers over the next four seasons, reaching a peak with 113 RBI in 1958 and 111 in 1959.

OUTFIELDER AL SMITH IS SAFE AT THE PLATE ON DALE MITCHELL'S GROUNDER. The throw from Yankee shortstop Phil Rizzuto was a bit too late in this 1953 game. Alphonse Smith (not to be confused with Alfred Smith, who pitched for the Tribe from 1940 to '45) played both third base and left field and batted a career .272 for the Indians. His best campaign was the pennant-winning season of 1954, when he hit .306 with 22 home runs and 77 RBI. Traded to the White Sox before the 1958 season, he played well there for five years before his career began to wind down with brief stops in Baltimore, Cleveland again (1964), and finally Boston.

LOU BOUDREAU AND EARLY WYNN. Boudreau, now manager of the Boston Red Sox, chats with contract holdout Wynn during a spring training swing in Sarasota in February 1953. Neither in Boston, where his record over three seasons was 229-232, nor in later managerial stints with the Kansas City Athletics and the Cubs, did Boudreau fare nearly as well as he had while playing for and managing the Indians from 1941 to 1950. His jersey, No. 5, was retired in 1970.

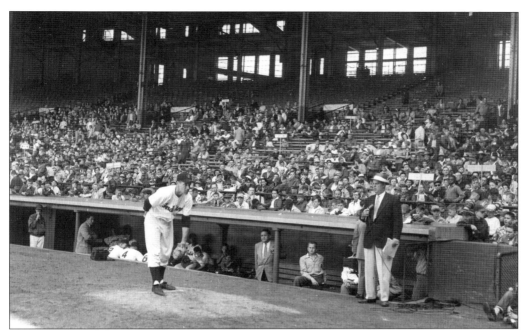

YOUTH SPRING BASEBALL CAMP AT MUNICIPAL STADIUM, MAY 1954. Bob Feller gives a pitching demonstration for 3,500 focused young baseballers. Players from both the Indians and the Detroit Tigers showed off their skills in a session which brought the six-week camp to an inspiring close. Frank Gibbons is the commentator.

AL ROSEN (LEFT), TED WILLIAMS, MICKEY VERNON, AND MICKEY MANTLE AT THE 1954 ALL-STAR GAME.

EARL AVERILL AND MEL HARDER, 1953. Tribe pitching coach Harder (right) had had a stellar career as an Indians pitcher, appearing in 582 games and posting a 223-186 record from 1928 through 1947. He often stymied great hitters such as Ted Williams and, especially, Joe DiMaggio. Gifted at developing young pitchers, he stayed with Cleveland as a coach for 16 years after his playing days were over. A fine gentleman and one of the club's all-time greats, his renown and popularity have been equaled by very few Indians players of any era. His jersey, No. 18, was retired in 1990, but the late Harder still awaits election to the Hall of Fame.

JACKIE ROBINSON AND WILLIE MAYS AT THE ALL-STAR GAME IN CLEVELAND STADIUM IN 1954. When Larry Doby came to the Indians, he strongly but unsuccessfully advised the club to sign Mays and two other Negro league stars, Ernie Banks and Hank Aaron. Imagine the 1950s in Cleveland if all three future Hall of Famers had joined the team!

Opposite: **YANKEES OUTFIELDER HANK BAUER IS SAFE AT THE PLATE AS HAL NARAGON TRIES FOR THE PUTOUT IN JUNE 1954.** After a brief stint with the Tribe in 1951, during which he played in three games, Naragon made the major league roster beginning in 1954. Limited to backup duty behind the superb Jim Hegan, Naragon was a fine catcher and game-caller, and a better hitter than Hegan (although his at-bats were far fewer). He was traded to the Senators in 1959.

WALLY WESTLAKE CROSSING THE PLATE AFTER A HOME RUN IN 1954. Al Rosen has scored ahead of him, and Dave Philley waits to bat. After Westlake played five and a half seasons in the National League, Cleveland purchased his contract from Cincinnati in mid-1952. As a role player in the outfield, he made few major contributions until the pennant-winning 1954 season, when he rapped some timely pinch hits. He was traded to Baltimore in 1955, and retired in 1956.

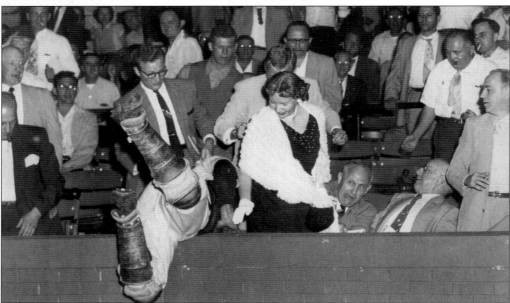

YOGI BERRA GOES AFTER JIM HEGAN'S POPUP, BUT MISSES, IN AUGUST 1954. August was the pivotal month in the Indians' quest to dethrone the "five-peat" AL champion Yankees. The Tribe's superlative play during the middle of the month, including a nine-game winning streak, gave them breathing room over New York. Cleveland's 111-43 record surpassed the 1927 Yankees' AL-record win total by one game, and the Indians' record stood until the Yankees 114-48 effort in 1998 (over a 162-game season), and then again the Seattle Mariners' 116 wins in 2001. But the 1954 Tribe's 154-game winning percentage of nearly .721 is still better than either of the later teams.

THE POLO GROUNDS ON THE EVE OF THE WORLD SERIES, SEPTEMBER 28, 1954. The Tribe, fresh off their best-ever regular season, prepares to face the New York Giants in the World Series, which would start the next day.

SPRING TRAINING IN TUCSON, MARCH 1, 1955. Indians traveling secretary Spud Goldstein has reached agreement with Larry Doby on a new contract.

TENSION FOR MANAGER AL LOPEZ DURING THE SEVENTH INNING OF GAME ONE IN THE 1954 SERIES. The score had been tied 2–2 since the third inning. In the eighth, Vic Wertz hit a 460-foot fly ball to deep center which seemed sure to push two runners across the plate, but Willie Mays somehow ran under the ball and snagged it. Larry Doby advanced to third, but Giants reliever Don Liddle retired the next two batters and kept the game tied. Pinch hitter Dusty Rhodes entered the game in the 10th and hit a three-run homer to beat the Indians.

TRIS SPEAKER WITH WILLIE MAYS AT THE 1954 WORLD SERIES. While Mays' spectacular catch in Game One did not in itself break the Indians' back, it was an omen of disaster. After a 111-win regular season, the Tribe was expected to flatten the Giants, but surprisingly it was the Indians who went quietly.

HERB SCORE PITCHING IN MAY 1955. Score threw harder than all but a handful of pitchers in the history of the sport. A brilliant young talent with a work ethic to match, Score seemed destined to anchor a winning Indians' staff for years to come, but fate cruelly intervened two years later.

EX-INDIANS OWNER BILL VEECK AND LARRY DOBY IN 1955. When Doby was new to the league in 1947, Veeck counseled his young player to turn the other cheek in the face of prejudice and hatred, but also supported him at every turn. The two became close friends and remained so until Veeck's death in 1985. Two years before this photo was taken, Veeck, then the owner of the St. Louis Browns (and in financial trouble), had been forced out of baseball by his fellow owners. He tried unsuccessfully to purchase other teams before becoming the owner of the White Sox in 1959—and winning the pennant.

HERB SCORE LIES GRAVELY INJURED. After being struck in the eye by a rocket off the bat of the Yankees' Gil McDougald on May 7, 1957, Score is surrounded by his teammates as well as trainer Wally Bock (bending over him). Remarkably, Score returned to pitch the following season, but arm problems and difficulties with pitch location greatly shortened the brilliant career of the lefthander. Subsequent generations know Herb better as a genial and dedicated longtime Indians radio broadcaster who retired after the club's gut-wrenching World Series loss to the Florida Marlins in Game 7, 1997.

JOE ALTOBELLI AND BOBBY AVILA IN 1955. Second baseman Avila (right) drove in first baseman Altobelli with a fly ball to win a late April game in the 17th inning over Washington. The Indians had a fast start that spring, then roller coastered to sixth place and up again to first by late August, before the Yankees gradually wore them down in September. Avila batted .304 and scored 76 runs.

MANAGER AL LOPEZ WITH CASEY STENGEL IN SEPTEMBER 1956. Lopez, brought in by GM Hank Greenberg to replace Lou Boudreau, went 570-354 over six seasons for a .617 winning percentage, the best ever for a Tribe manager. Apart from the 1954 pennant-winner, his Indian teams finished second to the Yankees each year until, after the 1956 season, Lopez resigned, citing stress and disappointment. He went on to manage the White Sox for nine full seasons and parts of two others, winning the pennant in 1959 but losing to the Los Angeles Dodgers. He was enshrined in the Hall of Fame in 1977.

MANAGER JOE GORDON ABOUT TO BE EJECTED BY UMPIRE ED RUNGE, AUGUST 1958. In his two and a half seasons as manager, Gordon (generally a gentle person) had personality conflicts with certain players and especially with General Manager Frank Lane, who additionally undermined Gordon's reign with a series of stunning transactions including the trades of Rocky Colavito and Herb Score. As a fitting climax to a turbulent period of .500 ball, Lane sent Gordon to the Tigers in exchange for their manager Jimmy Dykes—the only managerial "trade" in major league history.

FRANK "TRADER" LANE AT THE PIANO, NOVEMBER 1957. If he seemed genial here, he would soon show a very pugnacious streak, and his treatment of players was similarly brusque. Standing, from left to right, are Jim Hegan, Hal Naragon, Ray Narleski, and Mike Garcia.

78

TITO FRANCONA CONGRATULATES BILLY MARTIN ON A HOMER, JUNE 1959. Martin, who played one season for the Indians and platooned at second base, was one of two players with whom manager Joe Gordon had recurring problems. A decade before the beginning of his own tumultous managerial career, Martin's feisty and combative personality—manifested in several fistfights with opponents—was well-developed.

MICKEY MANTLE BEATS OUT A SINGLE AS VIC POWER RECEIVES THE THROW IN AUGUST 1959. Although the Yankees were frustratingly just a little better than the Indians through most of the decade, it was the pennant-bound Chicago White Sox whose four-game sweep of the Tribe at the end of August that would essentially knock them out of the AL pennant race.

HANDSHAKES AFTER A VICTORY IN JUNE 1963. Pictured from left to right are third baseman Max Alvis, catcher Joe Azcue, pitcher Ted Abernathy, and first baseman Joe Adcock. Scenes such as this were too rare in a dismal 79-83 season.

FIVE

The 1960s

On December 6, 1959, first baseman Norm Cash was acquired from the White Sox in a seven-player deal, but he needn't have bothered to report to spring training. On April 12, Frank Lane traded him to the Tigers, giving away 377 homers and 1,103 RBI in a career that would last until 1974. The impact of Cash's departure (like that of Roger Maris) would not be immediately felt, but five days later Lane outraged Indians fans by pulling the trigger on a shocking transaction that deeply wounded the team.

On April 17, just before the regular season began, outfielder Rocky Colavito was sent to Detroit in exchange for Harvey Kuenn in one of the worst deals in club history. Kuenn was a fine player, but he was older than Colavito, his legs were nearly shot, and even in his prime he had never been a power hitter like Rocky. With the city up in arms over the deal, a lesser aftershock occurred the next day when pitcher Herb Score was shipped to the White Sox. The Tribe reverted to 1957-58 form, finishing in fourth place at 76-78. Kuenn batted .308 but with little power, missing part of the second half of the season due to injury.

On August 3, Lane again stunned the major leagues by trading manager Joe Gordon to Detroit for Tigers skipper Jimmy Dykes (since managers cannot actually be traded, both were fired and rehired). The swap made no difference to either team's performance. In a fitting conclusion to the Colavito fiasco, Lane traded Kuenn to San Francisco on December 3, and then he himself took a job with the Kansas City Athletics.

In April 1961, Gabe Paul was hired as general manager, beginning a humdrum tenure that would last seemingly forever. With expectations lowered, the Indians (playing a 162-game schedule for the first time) started slowly, climbed into contention in mid-May, and actually led the league for a week in June before they collapsed, finishing the season at a .400 clip and ending up 78-83, thirty and a half games back. Paul fired Dykes at the end of the season and replaced him with first base coach Mel McGaha. Things continued in much the same manner in 1962, with the Tribe in the race until the All-Star break before a 33-46 finish mired them in sixth place at 80-82. McGaha followed Dykes out the door at season's end, and Birdie Tebbetts took over.

The contending teams of the 1950s were still fresh in memory, and with a new manager and a promising young group of players, there were higher expectations for the 1963 team. But the talent had been overrated, and injuries paved the way to a dreary 79-83 finish. Early Wynn, a 299-game winner, was reacquired by the Tribe. His quest for one more win (which took five starts) provided some small distraction from the losing and sold a few extra tickets, but not enough to make a dent in the $1 million that the Indians lost that season (and which necessitated the cost-cutting trade of pitcher Mudcat Grant to the Twins the following June). Things would not improve in 1964. Birdie Tebbetts had a heart attack during spring training, forcing Coach George Strickland into the leadership role for several weeks, and the team finished with the same record as in '63. There were some bright spots: outfielder Vic Davalillo won a Gold Glove, and young pitchers Sam McDowell (who had been up briefly in 1963) and Luis Tiant came up from the minors and went 11-6 and 10-4, respectively.

In January 1965, another fan favorite was brought back to sell some tickets. Rocky Colavito, all but one of his best years behind him, returned in a lopsided deal for three young talents which was as damaging as the 1960 trade that had sent him away. For one season it made sense because

Colavito's presence on the team helped spark a 282,000 gain in attendance compared to 1964, but catcher John Romano, outfielder Tommie Agee, and pitcher Tommy John would all go on to have fine careers for other teams, whereas Colavito would begin to decline after 1965. Sam McDowell continued to impress with a 17-11 record and a 2.18 ERA. The season began well but the team's play sagged after the All-Star break, and although the record of 87-75 was the best since 1959, it still left the Tribe in fifth place. It was the best year of Tebbetts' managing tenure, too, because the 1966 squad slumped to a .500 finish after a 10-1 start and a strong first two months (the "June swoon" was a matter of routine now). Though McDowell was hampered by a shoulder injury, Sonny Siebert came on strong, going 16-8 with a no-hitter. Colavito fell off in batting average, but not yet power. Tebbetts, who had never been the same after his heart attack, resigned on August 19, and Strickland again took over, with no more success this time around. Vernon Stouffer of the Stouffer food-processing empire purchased the team for $8 million, keeping Gabe Paul as general manager. Paul, however, made what he later acknowledged as a blunder by declining to hire former Indian great Bob Lemon as manager, opting instead for Joe Adcock, another ex-Tribe player—but a man who would irritate his players more than any manager since Oscar Vitt.

A story which would develop into one of the most interesting subplots of that era began on June 4, 1967, when first baseman Tony Horton, an intense and highly self-critical ticking time bomb, arrived in a trade with Boston. Meanwhile, under the grim Adcock regime, the Indians sank to 75-87, their worst season in many years. The pitching went into the dumper, and the fans responded with the lowest attendance in the major leagues. Adcock alienated Colavito and fellow outfielder Leon Wagner by platooning them, and a disgruntled Colavito was finally traded to the White Sox (for scrap) on July 29. As the first autumn leaves were falling, the axe fell, too, on Adcock's head. Broadcaster Jimmy Dudley's contract was also not renewed and former Indians pitcher Herb Score replaced him in the radio booth to begin a thirty-year tenure.

With former major league outfielder Alvin Dark installed as manager in 1968, a new attitude prevailed and the team got off to a good start. Sam McDowell rebounded to 15 victories and a fine 1.81 ERA, and the team remained in contention for the AL pennant until August. The good results gave the impression among the public that things were headed in the right direction. Unfortunately, however, a hidden power struggle was underway in the front office between Alvin Dark and Gabe Paul. Dark would win this round, and before the 1969 season he began to act as a general manager, negotiating contracts directly with players and causing friction with many of them, especially Tony Horton. On April 19, 1969, pitchers Sonny Siebert and Vicente Romo were dealt along with catcher Joe Azcue to Boston for Ken "Hawk" Harrelson and very little else. It was a high-profile but disastrous trade that created a logjam at first base, started Tony Horton on his journey toward the brink, and significantly lowered the Tribe's talent level.

Cleveland fans would learn what real losing was like in 1969.

The '69 season brought a new wrinkle for major league baseball, as the old single-pennant-winner system was abandoned and divisional play instituted. Expansion had brought the leagues to 24 teams, and each league now had an Eastern and Western Division. The two division winners in each league would meet in a new Championship Series to decide the pennant. Naturally, this was done to help ticket sales, since with (theoretically) four races instead of two each September, more teams could remain in contention later in the season and fan interest would be increased.

None of this would be of the slightest concern to the Cleveland Indians in 1969. Harrelson refused to report to spring training until his salary was doubled to $100,000, and Tribe management knuckled under. Over the next two and a half seasons Harrelson, who was plagued by injuries and just about done in any case, would contribute almost nothing. Horton hit 27 homers and collected 93 RBI, but he was unhappy at being forced to yield first base to Harrelson. On the bright side, Sam McDowell cut down American League hitters in '69 with 279 strikeouts, his 18-14 record remarkable for such a bad team. But resentment felt by the players toward Dark destroyed his effectiveness, and a free fall left the team 46 1/2 games out of first place in the new Eastern Division with a 62-99 record.

Woodie Held hits a Home Run in April 1960. Right fielder Harvey Kuenn (left), catcher Russ Nixon, and third baseman Bubba Phillips congratulate the shortstop. Kuenn, the AL batting champion with the Tigers in 1959, had the bad luck to be the player for whom the popular Rocky Colavito was traded on the eve of Opening Day 1960. A once-speedy player whose legs were now injury-prone, Kuenn was on the downslope of his career, in contrast to Colavito who was in his prime. The fans, angry at Frank Lane over the trade, took it out on Kuenn by frequently booing him. After a broken foot late in the season, he was traded to San Francisco in the winter. He later managed the Milwaukee Brewers to within one game of winning the 1982 World Series.

Shortstop Woodie Held and Second Baseman Johnny Temple Turn the Double Play in Spring Training 1960. Held had a fine season, leading the team in RBI until he broke a finger in July and was was forced to sit out for several weeks.

KEN COLEMAN INTERVIEWS CENTERFIELDER JIMMY PIERSALL DURING SPRING TRAINING OF 1960. Coleman had a long and distinguished broadcast career with the Browns, Indians, and especially the Boston Red Sox.

JIMMY PIERSALL EXECUTES A SLIDE IN SPRING TRAINING 1960. A two-time All-Star with the Red Sox, Piersall came over to the Indians in a trade before the 1959 season. His combative, outspoken nature made life difficult for managers Joe Gordon and Jimmy Dykes. He remained a productive player, though, batting .282 in 1960 and .322 in 1961, before winding down his career with three other teams from 1962 to '67.

FANS OUTRAGED AT GENERAL MANAGER FRANK LANE. Whether it was for trading away Rocky Colavito, Herb Score or future Hall-of-Famer Early Wynn, or for the infamous "manager swap," Cleveland fans hated Lane. The only people who liked him were the general managers of opposing teams who benefited so richly from his foolish transactions, and the newspaper publishers for whom Lane generated so many garish headlines.

MANAGER JIMMY DYKES WITH FRANK LANE. A former player with a long losing record as a manager dating back to 1934, Dykes came to the Indians from Detroit on August 3, 1960 in Lane's bizarre "trade" of managers which sent Joe Gordon to the Tigers. His arrival brought no relief to the slumping Tribe. Over the next 218 games, through the next-to-last day of the 1961 season, Dykes' winning percentage was .472.

MICKEY MANTLE AT CLEVELAND STADIUM DURING A MAGICAL SEASON, AUGUST 1961. Mantle hit 54 home runs, while his teammate Roger Maris (another brilliant Indians talent traded away by Frank Lane) broke Babe Ruth's single-season record with 61.

Opposite: **1963 TRIBE COACHING STAFF.** Pictured from left to right are Elmer Valo, George Strickland, Mel Harder, and Manager Birdie Tebbetts. Former Indians catcher Tebbetts inherited a talent-poor and difficult group of players when he took over for the fired Mel McGaha (who had managed only one season, 1962). He had very limited success, complicated by a heart attack, which he suffered before the start of the 1964 season. Though he returned after three months' rest, his physical and mental comfort did not, and he was never quite the same. Tebbetts resigned in August 1965.

STOCKHOLDER GEORGE MEDINGER AND GENERAL MANAGER GABE PAUL AT SPRING WORKOUTS, 1962. Paul (right) was a central figure in the Indians' history for more than two decades. A master politician with a good pokerface, he rose to top management from public relations and ticket sales, rather than a baseball background, and he made himself invulnerable by acquiring part ownership of the club. His close-to-the-vest leadership and mysterious personnel moves, frustrating to sportswriters and fans, were often connected with his successful efforts to keep the team in Cleveland (and financially solvent) on several occasions when other cities beckoned.

DISCUSSION OF A POINT OF ORDER IN MAY 1963. Manager Birdie Tebbetts tells umpire Frank Umont that Orioles manager Billy Hitchcock's giving instructions to pitcher Milt Pappas from the dugout should count as a trip to the mound. A second visit, of course, brings automatic removal of the pitcher.

"SUDDEN" SAM MCDOWELL THROWING FOR COACH ELMER VALO IN SPRING TRAINING 1964. McDowell's is one of the most fascinating Indians careers from the 1960s. He had blazing stuff and tremendous durability, but recurring problems with temper, concentration, and (beginning in his third season) drinking limited his effectiveness. Still, he won a lot of games and was often thrilling to watch on the mound. After the end of his playing days, he beat his alcoholism and became a sports psychologist, reestablishing a sterling reputation.

EMERGENCY IN TUCSON. The Tribe trained in Tucson, Arizona from 1947-92. After five inches of snow fell on Hi Corbett Field on February 3, 1964, the grounds crew tried to wash it away with a water hose. The less-than-acceptable results are seen here.

AN INDOOR SOLUTION TO THE PROBLEM. The Indians' workouts that day were held in the gymnasium at nearby Davis Monthan Air Force Base.

ANOTHER INDIAN WHO GOT AWAY: DETROIT FIRST BASEMAN NORM CASH. Frank Lane's trade of Cash to the Tigers on April 12, 1960, was a terrible transaction; Cash went on to hit 377 homers over the next fifteen seasons. In the 11th inning of this March 1965 contest, Cash chases a wild throw off a Chico Salmon hit to shortstop Dick McAuliffe. Salmon reached safely, setting up the winning run.

ROCKY COLAVITO AND FRANK LANE, 1965. Thanks to Lane, Colavito had given the best years of his career, and 173 home runs, to Detroit and Kansas City. By the time that Rocky returned to Cleveland in a costly trade made by Gabe Paul, ex-Tribe GM Lane (who had infamously traded away Colavito at his peak) was working as a scout. Despite the smiles in this photo, there was very little rapport between the two men.

THE RETURN OF ROCKY COLAVITO, 1965. Although Rocky is usually thought of as having been past his prime when he was traded back to the Tribe, in his first season back he put up excellent numbers: .287, 170 hits, 26 home runs, and 108 RBI. He still hit 30 homers in 1966, but his average and RBI dropped off significantly.

LEON WAGNER CONGRATULATES ROCKY COLAVITO ON A HOME RUN IN APRIL 1965. These two would become disgruntled in 1967, when manager Joe Adcock insisted on platooning them in the outfield. This misuse of the slugger was the final straw under a manager he disliked, and Colavito asked to be traded. On July 29, 1967, he was sent to the White Sox, ending an era—again.

DICK HOWSER AND LARRY BROWN, SPRING TRAINING 1965. Howser (with ball), the American League Rookie of the Year with Kansas City in 1961, came to the Tribe in 1963 in exchange for Doc Edwards and cash. Unfortunately, injuries prevented Howser from contributing much as an infielder over his four seasons in Cleveland, but he made his mark as an inspirational manager for the Kansas City Royals from 1980 until he lost a courageous struggle with brain cancer in 1987, a year and a half after winning the World Series with the Royals.

CATCHER DUKE SIMS DOESN'T LIKE THE CALL, 1966. Umpire Bill Kinnamon ruled that a ball hit by Baltimore outfielder Russ Snyder (who would play for Cleveland in 1968 and '69) stayed fair.

VERN FULLER SCORES THE WINNING RUN IN A 13-INNING GAME IN 1967. He is cheered on by outfielder Vic Davalillo. A light-hitting second baseman with a good glove, Fuller spent 1964 with the Tribe and then returned to the minors until being called up for good in 1966. The peak of his career came in 1969 when he was the starter at second for 29 games and batted .236 with 25 runs scored.

UMPIRE LARRY NAPP REFUTES MANAGER JOE ADCOCK'S ARGUMENT. Adcock claimed that pitcher Steve Hargan had been obstructed on the basepaths after a sacrifice bunt. Under Adcock's unsmiling leadership, the Indians had another gloomy season in 1967, going nowhere with a .463 winning percentage. He was fired after one year of his two-year contract.

UMPIRE BILL KINNAMON CALLS VIC DAVALILLO OUT AS THE ORIOLES' ANDY ETCHEBARREN HOLDS ON TO THE BALL, 1967. A contender for Rookie of the Year in 1963, Davalillo was hit by a pitch from the Detroit Tigers' Hank Aguirre, breaking his arm. He never recovered his full hitting ability again over five seasons in Cleveland, nor in a well-traveled stretch from 1969–'80.

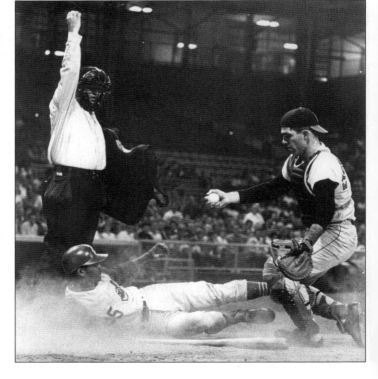

THE ORIOLES' DAVEY JOHNSON
LEAPS FOR THE HIGH THROW FROM
CATCHER LARRY HANEY. Tommy
Harper slides in for the steal. Harper
played for Cleveland only in 1968,
hitting .217 as the everyday right
fielder, until the Seattle Mariners took
him in the expansion draft. Johnson,
of course, went on to win the world
championship as manager of the Mets
in 1986.

VIC DAVALILLO CAUGHT IN A
RUNDOWN, 1968. After a suicide
squeeze failed, White Sox catcher Jerry
McNertney looks to tag or throw
Davallillo out. The batter is third
baseman Max Alvis, miraculously
recovered from a serious bout with
spinal meningitis, which had sidelined
him in 1964.

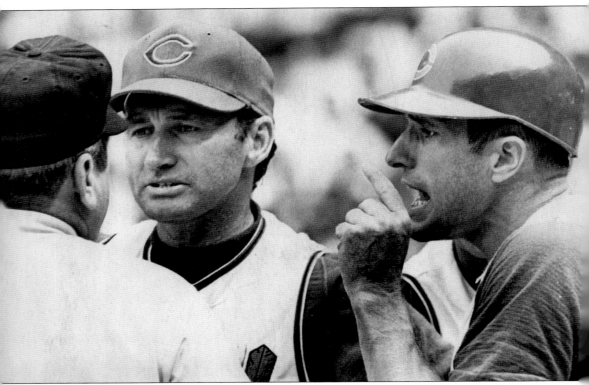

RESISTANCE IS FUTILE. In 1968, manager Alvin Dark and oufielder Russ Snyder argue to umpire John Rice (to no avail) that Snyder was safe at home.

ELMER FLICK CHATS WITH JOE DIMAGGIO AT AN OLD TIMERS' EVENT IN 1967. Flick, elected to the Hall of Fame in 1963, was on the Phillies' roster from 1898 to 1901, hitting .367 in 1900. After switching to the Philadelphia Athletics of the upstart American League, he played for the AL's Cleveland franchise from 1902 to 1910 and won the batting title in 1905. His career ended prematurely due to an unidentified illness of the stomach. Ninety-one at the time of this photo, Flick died in 1971.

ALVIN DARK WITH FIRST BASEMAN TONY HORTON, SPRING TRAINING 1968. The following season, Horton would become obsessed with trying to win over Dark, who was publicly critical of his skills during an ongoing salary dispute. The incredible intensity and perfectionism that drove Horton to play his best also, apparently, left him unable to enjoy even a fine individual performance such as his three-homer game in May 1970.

TONY HORTON AFTER BEING HIT IN THE HEAD WITH A PITCH FROM THE SEATTLE PILOTS' MARTY PATTIN ON JUNE 3, 1969. Horton regained consciousness and played the rest of the game. Just over a year later, however, the end came. Horton's fixation on proving his merit to Alvin Dark reached the breaking point when the manager pulled him for a pinch hitter on August 28, 1970. He had a nervous breakdown and, while still a young man with loads of talent, he quietly went home to southern California, never to return to baseball.

DAVE NELSON FIRES TO FIRST TO COMPLETE A DOUBLE PLAY AS TWINS OUTFIELDER BOB ALLISON SLIDES, 1969. Nelson played both second and shortstop over two seasons with the Tribe, 1968 and '69. He played eight more seasons with the Senators, Texas Rangers and Kansas City Royals, and appeared in the 1973 Al-Star Game. Nelson later served as a coach on Mike Hargrove's staff, and as a commentator on the Indians' radio broadcasts.

THE HAWK BALKS. Indians President Gabe Paul and Commissioner Bowie Kuhn confer about Ken Harrelson's refusal to report after being traded to Cleveland by the Red Sox in April 1969. A coveted acquisition for manager Alvin Dark, who had managed him briefly with the Kansas City Athletics, Harrelson had been a key player in Boston's 1967 pennant drive and an All-Star there in 1968. Harrelson made it known he would be a no-show unless the Tribe doubled his $50,000 salary.

HARRELSON IS ON BOARD. Indians management caved to the Hawk's demands, giving the first baseman the $100,000 he demanded. Trouble was ahead, as Tony Horton was already playing at first, and Harrelson (left) was not readily able to switch to another position. For all his movie-star-like appeal with the public, Harrelson did little to justify his salary. He batted a paltry .222 in 1969, and an ankle injury wiped out most of his 1970 season and forced his retirement in midseason of 1971.

Duane Kuiper Throws for a Double Play while Dodging the Orioles' Al Bumbry, 1977. A very popular player who was voted the Indians' Man of the Year for that season, Kuiper was a light hitter but a superb defensive second baseman. He tore up his right knee in 1980, but recovered fully after surgery and again played effectively late in the 1981 season, and for the San Francisco Giants from 1982 to '85.

SIX

1970–1982

By the 1970s, the Indians' old ballpark had lost its luster. In a cold, dirty, drafty Municipal Stadium that seated 80,000, only Opening Day could be expected to sell out. In the vast confines of the Stadium a crowd of 3,000 looked like 900, and in the quiet which usually prevailed, individual fans' voices (often with the most caustic commentary imaginable) could be heard clearly around the park. Those with seats in the row just behind the wide main aisle nearest to the dugouts, who had paid for what were theoretically excellent sightlines, found their view blocked by an unceasing procession of wanderers who promenaded back and forth all night, the same faces seen again and again, looking up into the seats rather than down towards the field. Who were they? And why had they come?

Perhaps they knew better than to watch the games.

In 1970, hope for recovery was provided by talented young players rushed up from the minors, including a great young catcher named Ray Fosse. Luis Tiant, who had faded badly during the 1969 season, was traded to Boston for third baseman Graig Nettles in a six-player deal. It seemed a good trade at the time, and had Nettles played his whole career in Cleveland it would have been. Sam McDowell went 20-12 and led the AL with 304 strikeouts, but his battery mate Fosse did not fare so well. In the 14th inning of the 1970 All-Star Game in Cincinnati, the NL's Pete Rose, racing for home to score the winning run, slammed into Fosse and permanently damaged the catcher's shoulder. Back in Cleveland, the team finished a mediocre 76-86. 1971, despite the Rookie of the Year honors earned by Chris Chambliss, would be a return to the horrors of '69 as the Tribe slumped to 60-102, the team's worst finish in 57 years. Alvin Dark, who had improperly negotiated several player contracts, was fired on July 30 by a newly-empowered Gabe Paul, and interim manager Johnny Lipon lasted only till the end of the season. On November 29 Sam McDowell was traded to San Francisco for Gaylord Perry and Frank Duffy. It was a good trade, as Perry would win the AL Cy Young Award in 1972 with a 24-16 record and a 1.92 ERA in 342 2/3 innings pitched, and Duffy would make a positive impact at shortstop. The flamboyant Nick Mileti purchased the club from Vernon Stouffer on March 22 for $8.8 million, retaining Paul as GM.

The strike-delayed 1972 season was another losing campaign, as the Tribe under new manager Ken Aspromonte was sunk by the familiar midseason slump. After the team finished in fifth at 72-84, Gabe Paul went to the New York Yankees as part of George Steinbrenner's investment group. Phil Seghi, no longer playing Robin to Paul's Batman, was promoted to General Manager; but the Yanks fleeced him in a November 2 trade which brought Graig Nettles to New York, where he would become a star. In 1973, the first year of the designated hitter in the American League, the attendance at the Stadium fell to the lowest in the AL as, with poor pitching, the team sank to 71-91. At the end of August Mileti stepped back to let limited partner Alva "Ted" Bonda run the organization.

Two more losing seasons were to follow. In April 1974, Seghi foolishly traded young Pedro Guerrero to the Dodgers for pitcher Bruce Ellingsen, who went 1-1 in his only major league season. Less than three weeks later Chambliss was sent to the Yankees in a terrible seven-player deal. Manager Aspromonte fulfilled the lame-duck final year of his contract, a 77-85 roller coaster to nowhere. The big event of the season was the disaster known as Ten-Cent Beer Night. On June 4, more than 25,000 fans turned out in anticipation of getting loaded on the cheap, and in the ninth inning a number of them stormed the field in a drunken riot, eventually causing a forfeit. Amid all the losing, Gaylord Perry did win fifteen straight starts and 21 games overall, while concealing a badly sprained ankle. But when veteran Frank Robinson arrived in a trade with the Angels in September, he and Perry interacted poorly, and it did not sit well with Perry when Robinson was named manager before the 1975 season.

Opening Day was often the "high point" of these losing seasons, but in 1975 true excitement was generated in the opener: Frank Robinson, in his debut as player/manager (and making history as the first African-American manager in the major leagues), homered off the Yankees' Doc Medich in his first at-bat. Things did not go so smoothly for Robinson the rookie manager, who was simultaneously feuding with Perry, learning to manage while under a microscope, and struggling with his own injuries. Perry was traded to Texas on June 13, and the team's tailspin turned around to respectability (and a 79-80 finish) after a closed-door meeting a week later. The second season under Robinson brought concrete improvement and the team's first winning season in eight years. Designated hitter Rico Carty brought some pop to the batting order, and Rick Manning would win a Gold Glove in the outfield. But after a strong start, three straight defeats by the Yankees cooled the team off and they fell from contention to a final record of 81-78.

Following the 1976 season the team went after new talent, but apart from a trade with Montreal for the classy Andre Thornton, their moves were disastrous. The free agent era had begun, and in November, Baltimore pitcher Wayne Garland was signed for what was then a staggering sum, $2.3 million over ten years. Garland promptly blew out his shoulder and would never throw another pitch without pain. The 1977 season began under a cloud as Carty shockingly undermined Robinson, questioning his leadership at an April fan luncheon. Although Carty was fined and suspended for 15 days, it was Robinson who would be fired by Seghi on June 19 and replaced by coach Jeff Torborg. Thornton emerged as an offensive force with 28 home runs, but the team staggered to a fifth-place 71-90 finish.

In February 1978, F.J. "Steve" O'Neill left the Yankees ownership group and purchased controlling interest in the Indians, bringing back Gabe Paul to serve as club president. John Lowenstein and pitcher Dennis Eckersley were sent away in lopsided trades, and pitcher Jim Bibby was lost to free agency via a faultily-drawn contract. The new ownership brought high hopes for improvement, but another dismal season ensued. After six painful starts, Garland had season-ending rotator cuff surgery, and the Tribe fared little better, winning just 69 games. The following July, with the team at 34-46, Torborg announced he would resign at season's end, but management decided that immediately would do, and promoted coach Dave Garcia to manager. In more positive developments, Mike Hargrove arrived from San Diego in a June trade and shredded AL pitching as the leadoff batter, and third baseman Toby Harrah also had a strong offensive year. The team's improvement came too late to save the '79 season, but the recovery to 81-80 gave hope for the next season—a familiar pattern. The team would remain near the .500 mark in 1980 and '81. Amid many injuries, and a major strike that wiped out 59 games in 1981, fans could only cheer great individual efforts such as Super Joe Charboneau coming out of nowhere to win the 1980 Rookie of the Year Award, Len Barker's perfect game on May 15, 1981, and fine pitching from Dan Spillner and Bert Blyleven.

In June 1982, the *Cleveland Press,* the last of the city's daily afternoon newspapers, went out of business, stranding a large and dedicated staff, abandoning the Indians in midseason, and making Cleveland a one-newspaper town. And with that event, this photo history comes to an end.

In 1978, Gabe Paul dubbed Cleveland baseball fans a "Sleeping Giant," predicting that with a truly competitive team they would turn out in droves. He was right, but seventeen years too early. When the Cleveland Indians returned to winning form in 1994, the city's mighty passion for baseball awoke. The timing was magical. In that season the Tribe moved into spanking new Jacobs Field, just as they began to reap the delayed benefits of deep-pocket ownership and several years' investment in a quality farm system. Drawn by both the glamour of the state-of-the-art ballpark and an exciting young team of hungry ballplayers, the fans responded with a major league record of 455 consecutive sellouts. They were rewarded with six American League Central Division championships in seven years and two World Series appearances, the second of which stretched into extra innings in Game 7 before things finally turned against the Indians. Very quickly, all the losing seasons began to fade from memory.

It's too bad the *Cleveland Press* didn't live to see it.

CATCHER RAY FOSSE IS CONGRATULATED BY SECOND BASEMAN EDDIE LEON AFTER A HOMER, 1970. Fosse's story is a classic Indians tale of "what might have been." An all-around prodigy who combined superlative defensive skills with the ability to hit for power and average, Fosse (in his first season as a starter) lost much of what he had in one stroke in the 1970 All-Star Game in Cincinnati when Pete Rose infamously crashed into him in a successful attempt to score the winning run in the 14th inning. His left shoulder badly injured, the gritty Fosse returned two days later and continued to play, while his injury seemed to go unnoticed by others. For the rest of his career Fosse played well, but through pain, and he never recovered his old batting stroke.

BOSTON'S CARL YAZSTREMSKI TALKS WITH FORMER TEAMMATE KEN "HAWK" HARRELSON.
In a bad year such as the 76-86 campaign in 1970, with the Indians finishing 32 games out,
many fans came out partly to see great opposing players such as Yazstremski, a riveting one to
watch in his 23-season career. He was a three-time batting champion and won the Triple
Crown in 1967 (the last time that anyone has achieved this feat), and is in the Hall of Fame.
A superb left fielder whose stomping ground was the Green Monster at Fenway Park,
Yazstremski retired in 1983 with 3,419 hits and 452 homers.

GRAIG NETTLES CONFERS WITH COACH KERBY FARRELL, 1970. Nettles was one of many players who were traded away by the Tribe just before they reached their peak. A good hitter and an excellent defensive third baseman, Nettles was dealt to the Yankees after the 1972 season, since Tribe management felt that Buddy Bell was ready to take over at third. Bell was indeed a solid and talented team player who made his mark with the club, but Nettles went on to better things with the Yankees and San Diego, playing in five World Series and hitting 319 career homers.

GOMER HODGE'S FIFTEEN MINUTES OF FAME. Harold Hodge, nicknamed "Gomer" because his voice sounded like Jim Nabors' Gomer Pyle, was brought up in 1971 from a long career in the minors and hit safely in his first four at-bats as a pinch-hitter. Here he receives congratulations from (left to right) pitcher Rick Austin, manager Alvin Dark, and trainer Jimmy Warfield. He was as much renowned for his claim (after those four at-bats) of having a 4.000 average as he was for anything else in his major-league career, which fizzled quickly.

Opposite: **ALVIN DARK CONGRATULATES CHRIS CHAMBLISS AFTER A TWO-RUN HOMER IN JUNE 1971.** Chambliss was the AL Rookie of the Year in 1971. He was a rising star over his three full seasons in Cleveland, but after seventeen games in 1974 he was traded to the Yankees where, like Nettles, he became a major cog in the New York machine.

107

BEEN THERE, DONE THAT. Senators manager Ted Williams coolly regards excited Washington slugger Frank Howard after a three-run homer at Cleveland Stadium in 1971.

COACH ROCKY COLAVITO, OWNER NICK MILETI, MANAGER KEN ASPROMONTE IN 1973. After serving as the Indians' television analyst in 1972, Colavito (left) returned to the field as a coach for the 1973 season. He was a broadcaster again in 1974 and '75, and coached once more from 1976–'78.

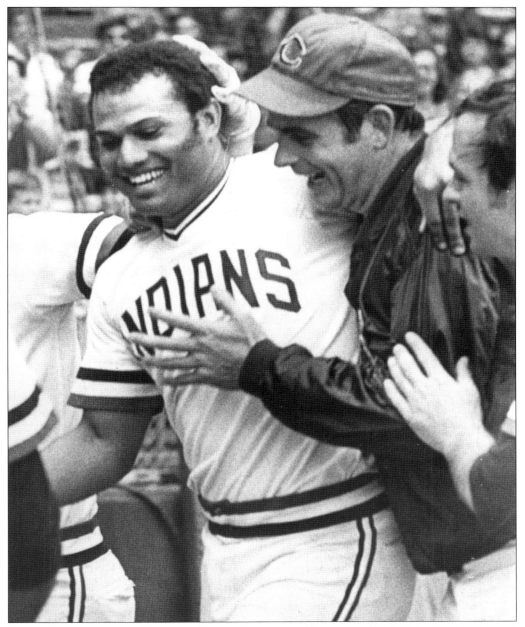

CHRIS CHAMBLISS AND GAYLORD PERRY CELEBRATE CHAMBLISS'S 10TH-INNING HOMER IN MAY, 1972. These two players were bright spots in an otherwise grim season. With a sterling 1.92 ERA, Perry threw five shutouts on the way to a 24-16 record. He was renowned for being a spitball artist, but in frequent shakedowns by the umpires he was rarely caught in the act. Perry was elected to the Hall of Fame in 1991, after a 22-year career with 314 wins.

TIGERS MANAGER BILLY MARTIN DISPUTES A CALL MADE BY UMPIRE RUSSELL GOETZ OVER A CHECKED SWING, 1973. After his playing days were over, the volcanic Martin began a storied managerial career, full of upheavals, which brought him to Minnesota, Detroit, Texas, the Yankees (five times), and Oakland.

NICK MILETI (RIGHT) AND PHIL SEGHI. Each man is shown in his customary cast of face, at the 1973 news conference announcing Seghi's being named general manager. While this was an apparent emancipation for Seghi (a career understudy), Gabe Paul's return from the Yankees in 1978 would again ease him into the background.

THE YANKEES' BUCKY DENT THROWS TO FIRST AFTER FORCING DUANE KUIPER AT SECOND BASE IN 1973.

TEAMMATES KEEP CHRIS CHAMBLISS FROM FALLING INTO THE DUGOUT AFTER CHASING A

Pop Foul, 1974.

113

OUTFIELDER OSCAR GAMBLE AND MILWAUKEE THIRD BASEMAN DON MONEY, 1974. A good .274 hitter over three seasons with the Tribe, Gamble is much better remembered today for his helmet-resistant hair.

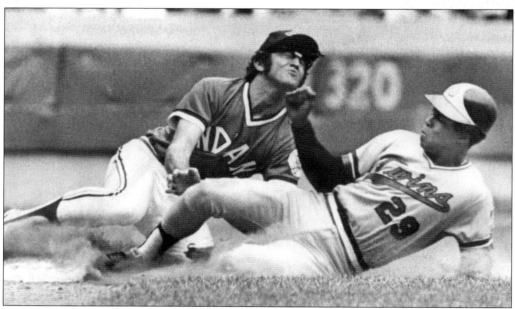

A FEARED OPPOSING HITTER. The Twins' Rod Carew seems to be, but is not, punching Cleveland utility infielder Ed Crosby while stealing third base in 1974.

A HOME RUN TROT INTO LEGEND. In his first at-bat as player-manager with the Indians, Frank Robinson cleared the fence on Opening Day 1975. Outfielder-designated hitter John Lowenstein offers enthusiastic congratulations. Robinson was under tremendous scrutiny, not only as a longtime star player and a first-time manager, but as the first African American ever hired to manage in the major leagues. His tenure was a difficult one, marked by clashes with veterans Gaylord Perry and Rico Carty, but his baseball knowledge was unimpeachable.

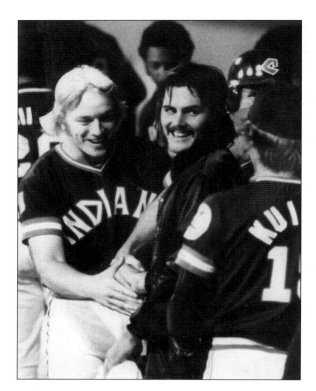

PITCHER DENNIS ECKERSLEY, AFTER A 1976 SHUTOUT, IS CONGRATULATED BY BUDDY BELL.

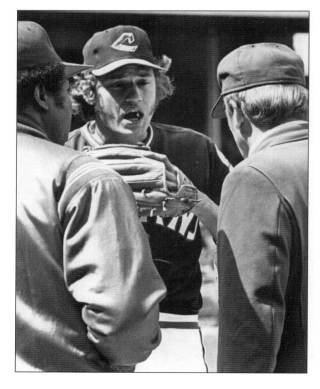

JIM KERN AND FRANK ROBINSON DISCUSS A BALK CALL WITH UMPIRE BILL KUNKEL, 1976. A colorful character, the hard-throwing Kern (nicknamed "Emu" after a gawky-looking species of bird) struggled to crack the Indians' major-league starting rotation. Tried as a reliever in 1975, he found his niche and saved 46 games from 1976–'78. Traded to the Texas Rangers before the 1979 season, Kern enjoyed one more fine season there before his career wound down with a succession of six more teams (including a final stop in Cleveland in 1986).

116

PITCHER WAYNE GARLAND BREAKS A LOSING STREAK IN 1977. Once perceived by fans as an overpaid, ill-tempered, complaining underachiever, Garland's courage in pitching for years through tremendous pain is now better appreciated. He was signed after one very good season as a starter for Baltimore, given a mammoth (for the time) ten-year contract as a free agent by the Indians, and suffered a major injury warming up for his first spring training game. Garland had torn his rotator cuff, and while delaying the inevitable surgery he continued to pitch, since he was determined to earn his money. But even after the surgery he would never regain his 1976 form.

JOHN LOWENSTEIN (LEFT) AND FRANK DUFFY CONGRATULATE DENNIS ECKERSLEY ON A SHUTOUT WIN OVER THE OAKLAND A'S. After three winning seasons as a starter with the Indians, Eckersley spent six more with Boston and three with the Cubs before he found his true calling with the A's. Manager Tony LaRussa recast Eck as a reliever and he went on to save 390 games for Oakland, St. Louis and Boston before retiring in 1998.

FOSSE AND ECKERSLEY ENJOY THE MOMENT AFTER THE NO-HITTER. While Fosse's physical skills were never quite what they had been before his injury in 1970, he was by all accounts a superb signal-caller.

DENNIS ECKERSLEY AND CATCHER RAY FOSSE AFTER THE LAST PITCH OF ECKERSLEY'S 1–0 NO-HITTER AGAINST THE CALIFORNIA ANGELS ON MAY 30, 1977.

SHORTSTOP TOM VERYZER COMPLETES A DOUBLE PLAY OVER TIGERS THIRD BASEMAN AURELIO RODRIGUEZ, JUNE 28, 1978. Cleveland was a four-year mid-career stop for Veryzer, who also played for Detroit, the Mets and the Cubs. He had a .966 fielding percentage in his twelve-year career.

PRINCIPAL OWNER F.J. "STEVE" O'NEILL AND TEAM PRESIDENT GABE PAUL, 1978. Both men had come from George Steinbrenner's ownership group in New York in February 1978, when O'Neill (left) purchased the Indians as the head of a group of investors that included Paul. General Manager Phil Seghi was left in the lurch by this transaction. He would again be relegated to a backup position, since Paul was taking over much of the work Seghi had been doing since being promoted to GM in 1973. Seghi had previously worked in Paul's shadow with the Cincinnati Reds and during Paul's first stint (1962-73) with the Tribe.

AN INJURED BATTERY.
Catcher Bo Diaz (fractured ankle) and Wayne Garland (arm surgery) compare ailments in 1978. Garland's surgery did not return his shoulder to full pitching strength, and though he soldiered on and showed occasional signs of improvement, he never achieved the form expected of him when the Indians made him a millionaire. He retired in 1981, his career a cautionary tale about the risks of signing pitchers to long-term contracts.

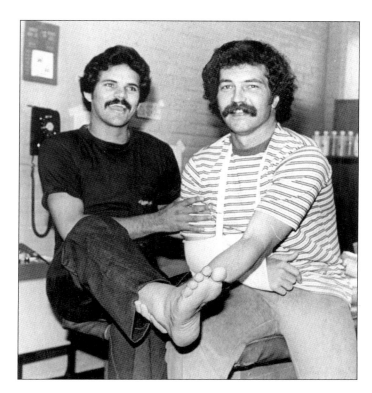

SID MONGE TIPS HIS HAT AFTER SAVING A GAME FOR LEN BARKER IN 1979. Acquired from the California Angels in 1977, Monge pitched very well in 1978 and especially 1979, when he won twelve games. His effectiveness fell off sharply thereafter, as he went 8–10 over the 1980 and '81 seasons before being traded to Philadelphia. He had better success there and, later, with the Detroit Tigers.

121

THE UMPIRE STRIKES BACK. Umpire Ron Luciano, calling Bobby Bonds out stealing, offers his signature "pistol" gesture as Royals second baseman Frank White makes the play in 1979.

RICK MANNING STEALS SECOND AS TEXAS UTILITY INFIELDER LARVELL BLANKS TAKES THE THROW, 1979. Manning covered tremendous ground in the outfield but never lived up to his promise as a batter, due in part to injuries. Blanks, a former Indian, was well-known for having clashed repeatedly with then-manager Frank Robinson.

"Super Joe" Charboneau Hits a Three-run Homer in August 1980. Charboneau (center), who had been acquired in a trade with the Phillies in 1976, was brought up from the minors in 1980, played in 101 games, and created a sensation. His similarities to a young Rocky Colavito were impossible to overlook. Charboneau hit .289 with 23 home runs and 87 RBI, as compared to Colavito's .276 average, 21 homers, and 65 RBI in his own rookie season of 1956 (in 131 games). Charboneau's 131 hits also far outstripped Colavito's 89 in 1956. He endeared himself to the fans with his frat-boy ebullience and blue-collar lifestyle.

Charboneau Signs a New Contract. For a brief time Super Joe (here shown with team president Gabe Paul) enjoyed intense local fame, but in spring training 1981 he hurt his back while sliding headfirst, and he never recovered his swing or his upper-body strength. Released in 1983, he failed to catch on with the Pittsburgh Pirates and endured various injuries and surgeries as his body gave out. Much loved by fans for his winning personality and accessibility, Charboneau—a guy who once removed his own tooth with pliers and opened a bottle of beer with his eye socket—has remained a Cleveland favorite.

ANDRE THORNTON AND TOBY HARRAH CONGRATULATE BO DIAZ ON A HOME RUN IN 1981. Another Indian whose career took off after leaving Cleveland, Diaz exploded for 262 hits with Philadelphia during the 1982 and '83 seasons, reaching the World Series but losing to Baltimore. He repeated the feat with 263 hits for Cincinnati through the 1986 and '87 seasons.

FIRST BASEMAN MIKE HARGROVE AND PITCHER LEN BARKER AFTER BEATING THE YANKEES IN 1981. Although his best season with the Tribe was his 19-12 record in 1980, the tall and intimidating Barker is best remembered for throwing a perfect game against the Toronto Blue Jays on May 15, 1981. Cleveland Stadium held 500,000 on that cold night, if one is to believe everyone who claims to have been in the crowd.

JERRY DYBZINSKI THROWS TO FIRST TO COMPLETE A DOUBLE PLAY IN 1982. Brewers first baseman Cecil Cooper is the runner. Dybzynski played at third, short and second, and hit .238 in 242 games with Cleveland from 1980 to '82.

THIRD BASE COACH JOHN GORYL PROTESTS TO UMPIRE KEN KAISER, 1982. Goryl felt that Toby Harrah's foul ball should have been ruled a hit.

ONE OF THE INDIANS' ALL-TIME GREAT OPPONENTS. Paul Molitor scores the winning run on a hit by Charlie Moore in the 10th inning of a 1982 game, just beating Rick Manning's throw to catcher Chris Bando. Although he often put a hurting on the Tribe during his 21-year career with Milwaukee, Toronto, and Minnesota, Molitor suffered a blow of his own on August 26, 1987, when the Indians ended his 39-game hitting streak, just as they had Joe DiMaggio's 56-game streak in 1941.

THE FUTURE MANAGER'S GAME FACE. Mike Hargrove shows his disgust with a call by umpire Dallas Parks, after a ruling that the Mariners' Manny Castillo was not picked off first base in a 1982 game. If anyone in the last 30 years might be called "Mr. Indian," it is Hargrove, who distinguished himself from 1974–'85 (in Cleveland only for the last seven seasons) with his bat, glove and hustle. Working his way up through the coaching ranks of the Tribe's minor-league system beginning in 1987, he returned to the show in 1989 as first base coach and took over for fired manager John McNamara on July 6, 1991. Hargrove managed the team for nine seasons with class, loyalty to his players (sometimes to a fault), and an inner fire. One of the greatest disappointments of the Cleveland Indians' magical late-1990s run was that Hargrove didn't get the championship ring he deserved.

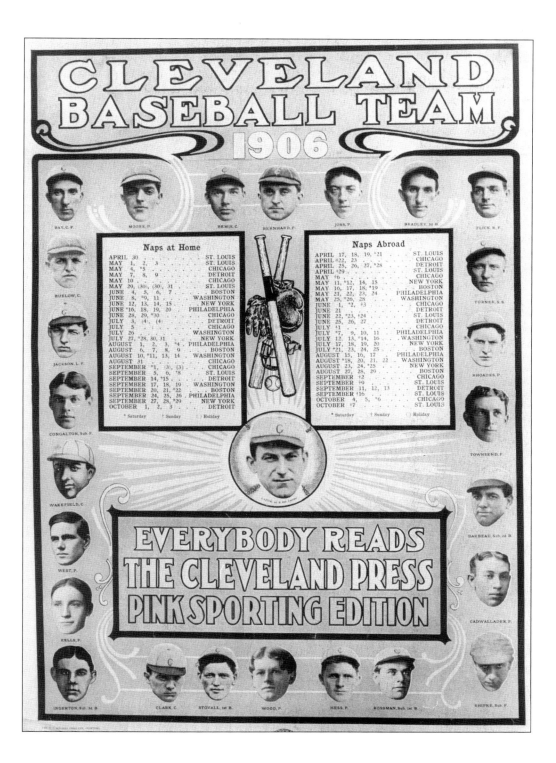